"I HAVEN'T SAID THANKS"

The story of

TED AND MOIRA HEATH

by Moira Heath

2

Copyright © Moira Heath 1998

ISBN 0 9534729 0 6

Published by Moira Heath 1998.

First Edition printed in 1998 by:
Hirst, Kidd and Rennie Limited, Union Street, Oldham, England.

"I Haven't Said Thanks"

Dear Reader,

This is a story of two people, very human, whom fate brought together from different worlds, who lived and loved through great heights and depths, the mountains and the valleys, and came through. One, Ted Heath, leaving behind a legacy of music that so many people today still love and enjoy and feel that it is a part of their lives, and the other, Moira, who helps to keep the legacy and memory of her beloved husband alive.

It is dedicated to all the dear people, who have been an essential part of this story. The musicians and singers, the radio producers, the Decca Record Company, the promoters of concerts and importantly the fans, who I sincerely hope, will enjoy this book, as it is written for them. Last but not least, the family who have loved and supported me throughout my long life, and brought me much joy and pleasure.

Ted and Moira on the occasion of their Silver Wedding

Contents

Chapter 1

TED

In 1902, in Wandsworth, London England, on March the Thirtieth, William George Heath and Phoebe Mary (nee Watling) had a son. They named him 'George Edward' but subsequently he was always known as 'Ted'. Phoebe, who was born within the sound of Bow Bells, had left school at the age of thirteen, and was placed in domestic service. William had run away to sea at the age of twelve, and was a cabin boy on a wooden sailing ship.

Sadly, there are no records of his travels, but on his return home to England, he was apprenticed to a carpenter. During World War 1, he was employed by the London General Omnibus Company, cleaning the buses, which were returned from the front, filthy and riddled with germ laden infections from the wounded soldiers they carried. He caught sleeping sickness (encaphalitis lethargica) from this work, and from then on was an invalid, and eventually bed-ridden for the rest of his life. Ted's brother, Harold, eight years older than Ted, had served in the Army and was discharged with V.D.H. (Valvular Disease of the Heart). So Ted, at the age of nearly seventeen had to support his mother and father.

To regress, his father was a talented amateur musician, and had formed a brass band, the Wandsworth Borough Band, of which he was the conductor, and had written some of the marches they played. He was determined that his sons should play an instrument, Harold the trumpet and Ted, originally at the age of six, the tenor horn. Ted would play with the Band outside Wandsworth Prison on Sunday mornings,' and at Fulham Football Ground (hence his life long devotion to football and especially Fulham). He stood on a box, because he was so much smaller than the other players.

At nine years old, his father taught him to play the trombone. Ted was frightened he would never be able to play this difficult instrument, and said to his father "I'll never be able to play that thing", but his father was determined and strict, and shut him up in a room to practice on 'that thing' for two hours every evening. Something for which Ted had great cause to be grateful later on.

Ted went to Swaffield Road School in Wandsworth. He wasn't a very academic pupil and besides being very shy, he was somewhat lackadaisical. All his energies (not of his own choice) were taken up by his music practice. His interest in sport was, of course, football, because of his father's brass band involvement with Fulham Football Club. Ted's love of the club remained all his life.

Somewhere along the line, he must have inwardly learned and digested algebra, mental arithmetic and percentages, which proved of incalculable value to him in later life.

He was remembered as a gentle and kind boy. He never learned to swim, but was only too happy to help others, smaller than himself. He didn't really leave his mark at school, but since he made such a success of his life, they are very proud to name him as one of their best pupils.

He left school at fourteen years of age, to go to work with his father, riding on the back of his dad's tandem bicycle, half asleep!

He did make a marquetry wooden box, which survived many years, but got lost in one of the house moves.

His very young life was almost entirely absorbed by music, not only learning to play an instrument, but also gaining the skill to read and write music on top of a natural knowledge of harmonies

Ted, with his father's brass band, The Wandsworth Borough Band

Chapter 2

With the Great War coming to a close, times were very hard, and there was no work. Ted and a small group of his friends, decided to form a small street band and go out 'busking'. Busking, for the uninitiated, is playing music in the streets, and taking a hat around for whatever money the generous public would give them. Pennies, threepenny bits, sixpences (tanners) and shillings (bobs). They played outside London Bridge Station. They had a pitch there, which meant getting there very early in the morning, to establish their right, otherwise another busking band would take it from them.

On the day the Armistice was signed, they played in Trafalgar Square, in the euphoric atmosphere of crowds of people, celebrating the end of the war, and the prospect of peace and plenty.

They also played in the West End of London, outside the Palladium Theatre, where Ted was to experience some of the biggest successes of his career, many years later, and outside the Savoy Hotel in the Strand. One day, Jack Hylton, the most famous British band leader of that time heard them play. He was in need of a trombone player that night and offered Ted the job. Of such gestures dreams are made. Ted had to rush around to borrow a dinner jacket and tie, something he had never possessed, and played that night.

It cannot be said he was an instant success. He could read music well, but had never played dance music as such. The dream was a phantom, and he was out of a job again.

There followed a disastrous episode, playing with a band "The Southern Syncopaters" in Vienna, Austria. Ted, very young and innocent, among a band of hard drinking and some drug taking 'low life's', found his life unbearable. He wrote home an S.O.S. and his mother managed to scrape together the money to get him home.

Chapter 3

However, the dream of playing in Jack Hylton's band finally came true. Incidentally, a pure coincidence, Moira who used to go to concerts with her brother and sisters at the Albert Hall -queuing up for the gallery at a shilling a time - went to a concert Jack Hylton played there and afterwards went round to the stage door to get Jack Hylton's autograph. Ted, who was in the band, probably walked right past her, neither of them knowing that their futures were going to be inextricably joined many years later.

Ted's career greatly improved. He was becoming known as a first class trombone player and a very reliable member of any band he played with. He was always kept very busy doing session work and film music especially being able to read at sight the most difficult pieces of music. In fact, he could read music as if he were reading a book and when he became a band leader, he could read a score, hearing the sounds of each instrument in his head as if the orchestra was actually playing. A most remarkable gift and talent. He worked very happily for many years with Harry Bidgood, Jay Wilbur and on film music with Muir Matheson.

Chapter 4

During those early years, he married a local girl called Audrey Keymer, who worked in a gas mantle factory. A hard and physically draining job. They had two sons, Raymond and Bobby within a short time of each other. This proved to be a great strain on Audrey, who was not strong, but fortunately Ted's mother helped to bring up the two little boys. Ted's uncle Porky and Auntie Barbara were also great supporters.

Sadly, Audrey died, quite suddenly from a miscarriage and Ted was devastated. Phoebe, Ted's mother, was very interested in Christian Science and Spiritualism. Ted became very involved, seeking consolation. It didn't however lift his depression, which was severe. The two little boys were quite a handful and his mother was unable to do as much as she would have liked in controlling them, because of the helplessness of Ted's father, who by that time was unable to do anything for himself.

Ted, much against his principles, finally decided to send them to boarding school, not a great success, and Ted's depression was very deep, but his work meant everything to him.

Chapter 5

A year after Audrey died, Ted, who was working with Ambrose, the top band of the day, at the Mayfair Hotel in London, was playing for rehearsals for the cabaret. This consisted of Richard Murdoch (later to be well known as Stinker Murdoch with Arthur Askey on the BBC) and the Buddy Bradley Rhythm Girls, a group of eight dancers, considered the best in the country, all hand picked. Among them was Googie Withers (the understudy, because she was the tallest) later to become a very famous actress and film star. Eve Moore, who became the wife of Guy Gibson, the wonderful dambuster V.C.and Ann Graves, who married into the Hillman family and Moira Tracey. The dress rehearsal went on until 4am and naturally the girls were needing transport home. Ambrose, who always had an eye for a pretty girl, sent his band manager round to offer Moira a lift home, which she happily accepted. A Rolls Royce and the leader of the band - what more could a girl want? But - the next night Ambrose asked to take her home again, and she asked if he would mind dropping off her great friend, Googie Withers at the same time. He made a bit of a 'moue' but agreed. Moira then made sure that she was dropped off first and left Googie to cope - a bit mean, but Googie was bigger than her and a little more worldly wise. Googie swore she walked the last mile home!

The next night the two girls asked the band manager if any of the musicians lived their way and were taking other girls' home. He immediately said the trombone player had been asking if Moira wanted a lift and that he would love to drive her, Googie and another girl, Enid Wild home. That was the beginning of the Ted and Moira love story.

Ted on a broadcast with Jack Hylton – 1920s

Moira

Chapter 6

MOIRA

Moira was born in Medellin, Colombia, S. America on October 13th 1910. Her parents were Arthur and Olive (nee Ashcroft) Tracey. She was the youngest of four children. Three girls and a boy. Kathleen, Brian and Sheila were born within thirteen months of each other, February, March and April in consecutive years. Kathleen in Colombia and Brian and Sheila in Bath in England. Moira was, no doubt, a happy mistake three years later in Colombia.

It was a very primitive country at that time, but the living was good for people like the Tracey's. Arthur was British Consul in Baranquilla. He and his brothers Frank and Sydney founded a business "Tracey Brothers Ltd" dealing in exports and imports. They were also pioneers out there. They were responsible for the opening up of the Magdalena River, with tributaries running off the Amazon into the jungle which was virtually unnavigable in the hot season, when the water was too low for normal river boats. They came up with the idea of tugs and barges, flat-bottomed boats, which were in constant use on the Manchester Ship Canal to be imported to Colombia, which opened up the jungle areas.

Moira's father had wonderful tales to tell of the riverbed being solid with alligators and the South American Indians primitive living conditions. There were also regular earthquakes and the odd one or two revolutions!

An exciting and challenging life for three young men from England. Moira's paternal grandfather Michael Tracey had also been an adventurous man, spending a great deal of his life searching for gold and the Eldorado of his dreams in Colombia. Arthur had a share in a gold mine, which was not too prolific in gold, but his joy and delight was collecting the wonderful un-cut emeralds and having them made into beautiful jewellery for Olive, whom he adored. The emeralds in Colombia are considered the best in the world. The collection came in very useful later, to pay for the children's education.

As a matter of interest, Moira's maternal grandfather was an explorer missionary and one of the first white men in parts of Africa, known as "the white man's grave". An exciting and interesting ancestry.

As previously said, the living was good in Colombia for the Tracey's but for delicate gently brought up young ladies to travel to such a primitive country took a great deal of courage and love to be with their husbands. Olive and Isobel (Frank's wife) were wonderful examples of such courage.

The advantages were that there was polo for the men - Arthur had his own string of polo ponies - and a good social life for the ladies, with many servants and high born S. American friends and Olive had two nannies for the children. During the hot weather, the family and servants went up into the hills, where it was cooler. In fact, Olive, when pregnant with Moira, had to ride the last miles up to their house in the hills on mule back. Moira always insisted that she could remember that ride!

The children were bi-lingual, Spanish being the native language, and spoke only in Spanish to the servants. The nannies however, were English of the old school. strict and correct. The children were dressed in starched white dresses for the girls and sailor suits for Brian.

A delightful story of their childhood was regarding the only other white family living near by. The little daughter of their neighbours was considered by Brian, Kathleen and Sheila, (Moira was just a baby) as rather prissy. One day they decided to teach her a lesson. They gathered some eggs from the hens, sat on the wall, and threw the eggs at her. What they hadn't realised was the inevitable proof of their naughtiness. When her beautiful white starched dress was stained bright yellow with the egg yolks, panic struck them. They tried to wash the mess out under a garden tap, which of course only made it worse but one of the devoted native maids washed, ironed and made the little dress pristine again, and saved them from their fate, the wrath of their nannies.

On another occasion, Brian and the boy next door had a bet about something or other. The boy bet his pony, but lost, and Brian gained a pony. Arthur insisted that the pony "Tommy" should be returned but the other father said it was a debt of honour and that Brian should keep Tommy.

Some time later, Tommy proved his worth. Moira, then eighteen months old, had crawled into the polo ponies paddock and was surrounded by them. Her golden curls seemed to attract them, maybe thinking it was some different kind of corn, and they were nuzzling her head. Tommy moved and stood over her until she was rescued. She thinks that this is the reason for her fear of horses for the rest of her life.

The children had probably inherited their father's adventurous spirit. One day, they escaped the nannies and went down to where the native children lived. They exchanged their toothpaste for sugary sweets made from the raw sugar cane, under indescribable dirty conditions. The little 'piccaninnies' no doubt, enjoyed eating the toothpaste while the Tracey's ate the sweeties. Kathleen and Moira went down with typhoid fever soon after, probably as a result of this escapade. When the fever reached a dangerous height, they were put into a cold bath to reduce it, a kill or cure treatment, but it worked. They both survived the dread illness.

When Kathleen was a baby, she was the first pink and white golden haired child the natives had seen. They would genuflect to her, thinking she was Jesus. By the time Moira came along, they knew better!

Among Arthur and Olive's friends were several South Americans. One particular friend was called Alejandro Lopez. As the children grew older, and later in England, they were strictly forbidden to swear, so Kathleen used the name 'Alejandro Lopez' as a very effective swear word to relieve her frustrations. Brian's favourite expression was 'Hells, bells and buckets of blood'.
Another time when the children had been naughty, their mother smacked them with a soft slipper. Of course, it did not hurt, so Brian said "let's crawl under the bed and laugh" which they did. This cheeky gesture earned Brian a proper spanking from his daddy, who used his hand, which did hurt.

Olive was very fond of a parrot, which Arthur had given her as a pet. This bird was not kept in a cage, and when there was a slight earthquake, it would get into Olive's bed with her, and cower under the sheets. As she had taken Moira into her bed at the same time, the parrot, Moira and her mother shared the same comforting shelter. Again, Moira attributes her innate inability to touch a live bird, however sweet and beautiful they may be, to this experience.

She has also had a phobia about flying insects. The children captured huge stag beetles, put them in a tin with the lid loose, and hid them under their mother and father's bed. The stag beetles then rattled the lid off the tin, and flew around the room, much to the consternation of the parents.

The moths were enormous too and Moira, to this day, cannot stay in a room with a big moth or any bug flying around. A phobia inherited by Martin and Val.

Just before World War 1 broke out in August 1914, Arthur decided to send his family home to England. They rented a house near Bath in South West England, hired a governess and settled down to life in England. This proved to be a little difficult at first. The children would see some pretty flowers growing in people's front gardens and would pick them thinking they were theirs. These little pale blonde children did not realise at first that the flowers were the pride and joy of people who had tenderly grown them. They soon learned the ways of their new neighbours and made many friends.

At the age of six, Moira was sent to boarding school with her sisters, to Ansdell College in Lytham St. Anne's in Lancashire.

She was very much the baby of the school, and it did her no harm. Brian was sent to Dean Close School in Cheltenham. So the children were safe from the Zeppelin raids in London. Their parents had a flat in Gloucester Place in London where Arthur joined Olive when he could. His life, business and consular duties kept him mostly in Colombia.

The children were very imaginative and had given themselves secret names, known only to themselves. Kathleen's choice was 'Violet Wrothesley' a somewhat flamboyant name she considered very sophisticated, Sheila's was 'Sybil Wood' typically quiet and good, and Moira's for no known reason was 'Daisy Wilmot'.

When the little girls were their pretend characters they did not answer to their real names, and had secret romantic adventures and jokes. It must have been rather a trial for the grown ups, but a great joy to the children.

Incidentally, many years later, Daisy Wilmot reappeared as the name of Val's (Ted and Moira's daughter) little Yorkshire terrier.

**Kathleen, Sheila, Brian --
Columbia, 1910**

Moira, aged 5

Chapter 7

After the war, the girls were moved down to the south of England to a boarding school, 'Oakdene' in Beaconsfield, an exclusive girls school. Moira was then nearly nine years old. Brian went to Oundle in Northamptonshire, the famous boys' public school.

Moira's days at school were happy ones. She was a bright child, having been put into a form with girls a year older than herself. She was very good at games, playing in the first teams of Lacrosse and netball at the age of twelve, and was showing a lot of talent at dancing. In fact, she had been dancing from the age of three. At five years old, she was dancing 'en pointe' without blocked ballet shoes. Bad for the feet of such a young child, but there was no stopping her. She knew that she wanted to be a dancer, and nothing would change her love of dancing and her belief that it was her destiny. Ted always used to say that she stood in the fifth position to powder her nose.

During this period of her life, her best friend at school was Catherine Oldenshaw, a niece of G.K. Chesterton, the famous author and poet. He and his wife lived in Old Beaconsfield, and would invite 'Bubs' (Catherine) and Moira for tea on Sunday afternoons. This was a great experience for Moira. G K Chesterton was a great man in every sense of the word. Enormous in build, he would wear a big black hat and cloak, his voice was very deep and he was rather frightening. The two girls would play war games in the garden. They were British heroes and everybody else was the enemy. On several occasions G.K., who understood their games and imaginations would surprise them, grab them by their hair, and say in a gruff voice, "you are my prisoners" and would take them up the spiral staircase that led to his studio at the top of the house. He would then make up libellous stories about their head mistress, Miss Watts, which delighted them, and did wicked drawings of her, and read them chapters from his latest book that he was writing - generally the Father Brown stories.

Moira asked him to write in her autograph book, and he wrote the following:

"Dear Moira, it was very wrong to keep your album quite so long. But think what dreams its presence fired, what murder stories it inspired. That famous artist of your kin who did St. Thomas a'Becket in".

And he did a brilliant drawing of the knight with a blood stained dagger, a reference to the knight named Tracey, who was supposed to have killed St.Thomas a'Becket. Unfortunately, this page was stolen from the autograph book. A mean and lowly deed. Moira was writing quite a lot of poetry and G.K showed great interest, and gave her a lot of encouragement.

Moira's life was unusual to say the least. Her mother would pack up the children's things, send them off by train to school, and not see them again until the school holidays, which were spent in hotels.

At Christmas and Easter, she would take a suite of rooms in a hotel off Portman Square, hire a piano so that they would continue their practice on that instrument. Reserve seats in several of the theatres, so that they saw most of the shows, including the Russian ballets directed by Serge Diaghilev and the opera. In the summer holidays, they went to Jersey in the Channel Islands, again staying in a hotel. There was no home life at all. Their mother travelled in Europe to Paris, Aix Les Bains, Stockholm and Vichy and made no effort to make a home for her children or her husband who was in South America. It was a life style envied by their school friends, but was really a deprivation. Moira's friends would invite her to their homes, and she saw the kind of life that she was denied. They're own bedrooms, breakfast 'en famille' with porridge and bacon and eggs on the sideboard, the homely feel of families and pets, and their parents always there. This influenced her enormously and when she and Ted were married, home was the most important place in their lives. She devoted herself to making it a loving place for all her family, and one of her sons once said "Home is heaven".

Chapter 8

Life was not going smoothly for the Tracey's. Arthur had been very ill with yellow fever, but did not take his doctor's advice and return to the equable climate of England. He was working very hard to keep up the expensive style of hotel living and expensive schools. He then caught a bad bout of influenza and was ordered to return to England to regain his health. This was in the summer of 1923. Olive had made friends with people called 'Tanqueray' of the Gordon's Gin family. They mutually decided to take a house in Wissant, France for the summer holidays. This was fine for the children of both families. But the weather was cold, normal for that part of the world, and the sea was freezing. Arthur joined them and for the first time in years, he was enjoying getting to know his children. When they went down to the sea to bathe, he insisted on going with them. It was bitter cold, and the youngsters decided they had had enough. The older ones went on, back to the house, and Moira stayed behind, waiting for her father to dress. He was behind a rock and he was there a long time. In the end she said, "Come on daddy, we'll catch our deaths of cold" and there was no reply. She went round the rock and found him blue with cold, still in his swimming trunks and he had no idea where he was or who she was. She wrapped a towel around him and gently led him back to the house. He was desperately ill, a specialist was called from Paris and he was taken back to England to hospital. He was ill for three years before he died, in the Holloway Sanatorium in Virginia Water – coincidentally, where Ted's life was to end many years later.

Chapter 9

Money then became very scarce. Brian, Sheila and Kathleen left school to earn their living and Moira was kept on at Oakdene by Miss Watts, as a non-paying pupil. The intention was kind, but she was treated as a charity girl, and made to pay for the kindness in many small and demeaning ways. It really did her no harm, if anything strengthening her character, and taught her that life was not always going to be sweetness and light.

At the age of fifteen, through the encouragement of her dancing teacher, Maisie McDougal, she gained a scholarship at the Ginner-Mawer School of Dance and Drama. It was a three-year course, and although she was a year too young, she was accepted as being capable of completing the very strenuous and arduous course. This not only included Greek classical dancing, inspired by Isadora Duncan, but character, national and ballet, drama training and voice production and mime, but also written work, and attending lectures on History of the Dance, History of the Theatre, the Comedia del Arte, Greek Mythology and Anatomy for studying the treatment of injury and disablement in children. She loved every minute of it, and passed with honours.

During the training, she won the prize for her composition of dance and performance. The presentation was made to her by Anna Pavlova, one of the world's greatest ballerinas, who congratulated her, and said she had a great future. The music Moira had chosen was 'Clair de Lune' by Debussy. Ted had an arrangement made and recorded it for Decca, during his band leading years.

During the final year of training, it was a rule that every student should attend an audition in a theatre. It was arranged for Moira to go to the Holborn Theatre for an audition for a Christmas operetta called 'The Toymaker of Nuremberg', Frederick Ranalow and Hay Petrie had the leading roles and Leslie French, the eminent dancer was doing the choreography and producing the dancing.

Moira turned up with all her music and dancing gear, ballet shoes, Russian boots, Greek tunic, tambourine etc. etc. She got lost trying to find her way back stage, and finished up in the upper circle. She heard them say "Thank God that's the lot" and terrified that she was going to miss the audition, she piped up "what about me?" They laughed and said "stay where you are" and sent someone to fetch her down. They decided they would have some fun, after seeing one hundred and twenty applicants for the job, with this innocent little girl. They let her go through her whole repertoire, ballet, Russian, Italian plus the Greek friezes and tragedies, and then said, "can you sing?". Breathless, she said "no" and they said, "that's all right darling. You are one of the first to be chosen", and she was given one of the solo dance parts. It was a wonderful start to her professional career, and made her decide that the stage was her dream come true, and teaching dancing would be secondary.

She did however start to teach dancing, having already experienced it with Maisie McDougal and the money she earned had helped with her living expenses while she was a student. She had had enormous help from a charity called 'The Girls Realm Guild', which was formed to further the education of the daughters of gentlemen, who had fallen on hard times. They paid for all her books, dancing shoes and tunics, and towards her fees at Ginners. And she owed them a huge debt of gratitude.

She taught at a girl's school in Mill Hill, a convent run by nuns. The delight was when the nuns joined in, picking up their habits round their knees, and loving it She also taught at County Hall, London, for the London County Council. Evenings were for the young ladies from the Prudential Insurance, and Saturday mornings were for housewives. The girls from the Bank were terrifically keen, and a delight to teach. The housewives were something else. Keen yes! But fat or painfully thin, some with very little sense of rhythm and 'two left feet' but interested in everything and so enthusiastic, the classes were entertaining and fun.

Moira had to prove her British nationality to be allowed to work for the L.C.C. It so happened that she did not have a birth certificate. Her father had registered her birth as a British citizen within an hour of her birth in Colombia, but all the relevant papers were destroyed in an earthquake. Consequently, there was no official record of her birth. Olive, her mother had to go to the police station at West Kensington on a Monday morning to swear in front of a magistrate that Moira was born of British parents on October 13th 1910, and that she actually existed. This little piece of paper, duly signed and witnessed was important to Moira for all of her life. The only snag was that Monday mornings at the police station were mainly busy with prosecuting and fining the local prostitutes who had been taken to the cells over the weekend. As Moira's mother looked and acted like a duchess, in her sable fur and pearls, she was obviously rather a fish out of water! And a figure of some hilarity amongst the ladies of the night!

Chapter 10

For Moira, being in the theatre was a whole New World. She adored every minute of it, even when the other girls, who were older and more experienced, teased her in the dressing room. Their standard trick was to say "all virgins stand on their chairs", and then roared with laughter when the only ones to do so were Moira and a girl called Dorothy Holiday, another innocent. They remained friends for many years and Dorothy was Moira's daughter's godmother.

'The Toymaker' also opened up a new world of independence for Moira. She was earning a good salary, on top of which there was overtime for all the extra rehearsals. Up to then, the family had pooled their earnings and handed it all over to their mother who then doled it out as she thought fit. Even Brian had to do the same, and it seemed rather unfair that he never really had enough to take girlfriends out to special places. His life changed, when he was in the County of London Yeomanry during the Second World War - sadly he was killed in Italy towards the end of the war, as were so many young officers and men - such a short life.

To continue, Moira with her extra earnings, decided that she would save the money and buy Christmas presents for them all. This was the beginning of a small rebellion against her domineering mother which went on up to the time when Ted came on the scene.

Chapter 11

After the show closed in the February, life went on as before. She finished her diploma course at Ginners in the summer, and continued to teach dancing, but her main desire was to get back to the theatre. She heard that there was to be an audition at the Drury Lane Theatre for a new show called 'Cavalcade', by Noel Coward. This was an enormous production, entailing four hundred in the cast as 'crowd'. Moira was chosen, and when Noel Coward interviewed her, he told her that the pay was thirty shillings a week. She was horrified and told him that she earned more than that in one afternoon teaching. He said that there would be small parts given to people within the cast, and she would have the opportunity to apply for one of these. She asked him if she could go into a corner and think about it. He was highly amused and said "Of course, darling. You go and think and then come back and tell me your decision". Of course she decided to take it, but on the understanding that if there were to be Wednesday matinees, she could have the time off, to keep her teaching job. This small inexperienced girl was making a deal with the great man. From then on, during rehearsals, which were fantastic, he always called her "Moira" whereas the players in the huge crowd scenes were usually called by numbers.

Moira watched all the rehearsals of the star actors, sitting quietly in the dark auditorium and absorbing the magic of the theatre, and the consummate skill of Noel Coward, but she realised there were no dancing parts. When the time came for the audition for small parts, she turned up with her music, Debussy's "Clair de Lune" and her long Grecian tunic. Elsie April, who was Noel Coward's, personal pianist told her gently that there was no part for dancing – Moira, with her strong belief in herself said "But I would like to show what I do best. Please let me dance" and so she did. Fate was on her side. Watching the audition was Leonide Massine, famous dancer and choreographer of the Russian ballet, Charles B. Cochran, the great entrepreneur who was putting on a big production of 'Helen' and A.P. Herbert who was writing the 'book' of Helen and Max Rhinehart who was composing and arranging the music. Massine immediately said, "I want that girl", and Moira's dream was to come true.

Noel Coward was kindness itself, and said she could stay in the cast of 'Cavalcade' until rehearsals began for 'Helen'. This was a most wonderful experience. Cavalcade was enormous. The stage at Drury Lane had many lifts and elevations and there were scenes in the show that were breathtaking. Troops leaving a station on a steam train, the engine actually on stage, a theatre auditorium on the stage. Audience looking at audience across the orchestra pit, Brighton beach, with a raised promenade and a magnificent ballroom scene and a scene on the Titanic, the night before she was sunk by an iceberg. Only a genius like Noel Coward could conceive and produce a stage production like this - much, much better than the film produced years later.

In the first six weeks, they played to all the crowned heads of Europe, and Moira was privileged and lucky enough to be, albeit, a very small and insignificant part of it.

Chapter 12

The rehearsals for Helen started. Another magnificent production with a dream cast - Evelyn Laye as 'Helen', George Robey as 'Menelaus' and the great and wonderful dancer Massine to choreograph and produce the ballet. It was another joyous experience for Moira. Massine had taken a liking for her and chose her for several special movements. At one time, rehearsals being hard and exhausting, Moira had crept away, and gone to sleep on 'Helen's' bed! A beautiful creation by Oliver Messell, who did the exquisite decor. It had a figure of Leda and the Swan at its head and a white (imitation) fur bed cover. Massine, who found it difficult to pronounce 'Moira', would say, "Where's that Tracey. I want her", and she would be dragged on to the stage, guilty but refreshed. A wonderful time for her, never to be forgotten.

Chapter 13

After the run of Helen, which lasted nearly two years, ballet drifted out of fashion, and there was very little work. During that time, Moira was teaching and being courted by nice young men. One afternoon, she was taken to the Savoy Hotel for a tea dance. Afterwards, she and the boyfriend were walking through Trafalgar Square looking for a taxi, when crossing the road she was struck by a large lorry, sent flying and after turning two somersaults, landed on the road. A crowd gathered round and the very young driver of the truck, white faced and frightened asked her if she was all right. Taking pity on him, she said she was, asked someone to get her a taxi, said goodbye forever to the boyfriend who had panicked and went home. As soon as she was in the taxi, she realised she was badly hurt. Her arm was broken, and the ligaments in her chest were torn, and of course she was badly bruised. The taxi driver was shocked, but she insisted she wanted to go home. Her mother nearly had a fit when she saw her, and immediately called a doctor. The pain of her torn ligaments was excruciating and hid the further damage that had been done.

It was only later when she was X-rayed that it was discovered that the base of her spine, the coccyx was broken. She was told that she would be in plaster for six months and it would be another six months before she would be able to walk, let alone dance. She was shattered, and asked what would happen if she did not have the operation to re-break her back. They told her she would suffer from a bad back for the rest of her life. This was not for her. She was determined to beat the injury. After three months of complete rest, she started gentle ballet exercises and despite suffering acute sciatic pain in her back and leg, she started dancing again. By that time, the top name in the dancing world was a young American, Buddy Bradley, who was producing the dances in many shows. But it was not ballet, it was tap dancing. Moira went to him for lessons. His standards were very high, the intricacies of his steps were difficult. Moira's mother, an old fashioned lady, insisted that while Moira was having her private lessons, the door should be left open, because Buddy was black. He was highly amused and from then on called her 'Chastity Tracey'. After three lessons, she was picked to join seven other girls for cabaret at the Mayfair Hotel. They were called the Buddy Bradley Rhythm Girls, each picked for their style and personalities and from then on, fate and destiny were bringing Ted and Moira together for the rest of their lives.

Chapter 14

Moira was fortunate to be at the right time and the right place during her young days. In 1932, she was chosen to work for John Logie Baird, the inventor of television, when he was experimenting with this exciting new development in the world of vision and radio. He had a small studio in Long Acre near Covent Garden, where the intensely interesting and important inventions took place. It so happened that he needed a dancer to perform in a 6 foot by 6 foot space, to further his work in visual movement pictures on a small screen. Moira was engaged by him for five shillings a day, to dance small and neat movements in this tiny space. Her make up was, to say the least, unusual. Her eyes and face lines were black as also were her lips, because red turned white on the television screen and her costume was a navy blue and white check skirt with a navy blue bodice. The floor was black and white checks. She looked grotesque in the daylight, but in the lights for the photography, the result was quite normal. Baird would say to her 'Quick Moira, come round here to the camera, your image is still on the screen', where it stayed for a brief moment. Little did she realise that she was helping in the process of making history. Television was to change the world of entertainment and news reporting.   Later, when the BBC took over the transmissions, she appeared in an internal trial at Broadcasting House. She asked for, and got, Eugene Goosens, the famous clarinet player to accompany her!

She was honoured to receive a bronze medal in recognition of her services to television at the Albert Hall in 1984.

Ted and Moira

Moira – Engagement Picture, 1933

Ted – Engagement Picture, 1933

Chapter 15

The driving home took longer and longer and Ted and Moira talked in the car outside Playfair Mansions, Queen's Club Gardens where Moira lived, sometimes until dawn and the milkman had started to deliver the milk. Moira's very irate mother blew her top.

During these conversations, Ted told Moira of his deep unhappiness at the death of his wife, and his worry about his sons.

Within two weeks, he had asked her to marry him. She was not ready for it, and thought he was giving her a 'line'. She had her dancing career, which was progressing well, and felt she was too young and inexperienced to settle down, take on a widower for a husband and a ready made family. Ted persevered, going entirely against his nature, waiting for her for hours, when rehearsals of the show went on longer than expected. Waiting outside the Cafe de Paris, a very famous fashionable place to dine and dance, into the early hours, where she went with Googie and boyfriends after work.

There is one rather charming story about that. The young party left the Cafe de Paris at about 2am (they had gone on after the show) and decided to go on to the Ace of Spades, an all night roadhouse, on the Kingston-by-Pass (now the A3) for breakfast. The 'in' thing to do. Ted followed them without them knowing (having waited patiently outside the Cafe all the time they were in there dining and dancing, until their car broke down at Robin Hood Gate. He watched them get out of the car and start walking the three miles or so to the nearest garage. The girls in long evening dresses and high heeled shoes. He then turned round and happily went home to a good night's sleep. He rang Moira up at eight o'clock the next morning and innocently asked her if she had had a good time. At last, his sense of humour was surfacing.

On another occasion, the girls were rehearsing for a show at the Strand Theatre, with Leslie Henson and Robertson Hare. They were given a long weekend off, and went down to Googie's mother's house in Swanage, Dorset for the weekend. That evening they were involved in a car crash. Fortunately no one was seriously hurt, but Ted, who had telephoned Moira the next morning, was much concerned to hear of it. A few hours later, he turned up, and demanded that he should take her home to her mother. Needless to say, Moira was not very pleased, and said he had no right to order her life. However, she took pity on him and said he could drive her and Googie back to London the next day, instead of them going by train. When the time came for him to drive them home, something went wrong with the car and it would only go into reverse. They drove backwards all through Swanage to a garage, and Ted had to put the girls on a Green Line bus for London. Poor, poor man. He was humiliated but it brought things to a head. He once again, begged Moira to marry him and they became engaged. Six months after they met, they were married.

Chapter 16

During the summer of 1933, Ted courted Moira intensely. Their first real 'date' was to go to Royal Ascot for the races. Ted loved betting with the bookmakers, never an enormous amount, but for the sheer satisfaction of picking a winner from the form book.

This first Ascot was an occasion for them both. They had lunch before the races, then Ted left Moira to watch the horses in the paddock, while he went down to the bookmakers to check on the odds and place his bets - Moira was very happy watching the horses parade, and picking her own winners, sometimes! She also was thrilled to see the Royal family, and other famous personalities. The most beautifully turned out lady and the most beautiful too, she considered to be the Begum Aga Khan, the wife of the old Aga Khan. She also saw Harry Roy with his lovely wife Princess Pearl, who was very pregnant - rather a surprise at Ascot, but typical of the flamboyant Harry Roy.

Moira wore an eau de nil outfit, with a hat to match. Years later after the war, Ted asked her why she didn't wear that hat again to the races!

From 1933 onwards, Ted kept the first day of the Ascot meeting free, so that they could repeat that wonderful first date. Only during the war, when the meeting was cancelled, did they miss going. Years later, when Ted was famous, a band of buskers outside the entrance to the racecourse called out to Ted: 'Whatcher Ted – Good luck to you and the little lady'.

Ted at Ascot Races

Chapter 17

Ted and Moira were married at Kingston Register office in December 1933. Moira was all in green, even her flowers were green orchids, defying superstition and her mother's disapproval of their marriage. After many tears and recriminations Moira's mother, brother and sisters did attend the wedding, and the small reception they had afterwards at the house Ted had bought for the start of their new life together. A foible of Ted's was to buy a house Moira hadn't even seen before he signed the deeds, but she was not worried. It was a beautiful cottage, called Oak Cottage. George Smith, the saxophone player, was his best man. George Smith later became manager of the Savoy Theatre. Max Goldberg, trumpet player, with Ambrose went along and took photos on a cine camera.

That night, Ted was working as usual. It was a broadcast from the Embassy Club with Ambrose. He drove Moira home to Playfair Mansions to spend the evening with her mother and family and left her there to listen to the broadcast, and then picked her up after he finished work about 2am. He had taken a crate of champagne for the musicians at the Embassy, and being hardly a drinker himself had a glass, or maybe two and 'fluffed' a note during the broadcast. This so upset him, he was always a perfectionist, he barely spoke to Moira for a week after! There was no honeymoon - both going to work on the Monday night. Ted to the Embassy, Moira to the Strand Theatre

The cast of the show that Moira was appearing in 'Nice Goings On' at the Strand Theatre with Leslie Henson and Robertson Hare, gave Moira a beautiful silver tea service presented to her on the stage, after the evening performance.

Oak Cottage, 1933 and Ted (inset) outside Oak Cottage, 1934

Chapter 18

Oak Cottage, Copse Hill, Wimbledon, was a very pretty timbered cottage. The downstairs was oak panelled with beams. A dining room and drawing room – Both had large fireplaces, the one in the drawing room was very big – almost possible to walk into. There were four bedrooms, and a pink marbled bathroom and they settled in happily.

Ted took his sons out of boarding school and they went to a day school in Wimbledon. The Wimbledon Common Junior Preparatory School.

Moira worked on at the Strand Theatre for two months after their marriage, but they found they were almost having to make appointments to see each other. The decision was made for them because Moira became pregnant. They employed a maid called Vera at the grand salary of £1 a week, of whom they became very fond and a member of the family. Martin John Tracey was born in Wimbledon on October 4th 1934 - he was a beautiful child and a joy to them.

Life at home had some problems though. Ray and Bobby had been running wild for a year before they went to boarding school and after one term, their behaviour and manners to say the least were rough. They swore at 'Grandma' Ted's mother, and reduced her to tears, Moira had never tried to take their mother's place, but she was young and inexperienced at looking after little boys. Many times, they would say "damn and blast you - you are only our step mother". This hurt her very much. The final crunch came when Moira, who in the last few months of her pregnancy had not told Ted of her unhappiness, was told by nine year old Ray "Daddy doesn't love you like he did mummy. You are only an outsider". This broke Moira up and she had to speak of her fears that the boys and Grandma would never accept her. Ted's reaction to this was one of total love. He told her he loved her more than he had ever loved before, and that she meant everything to him. He told this to his sons and his mother, and said they must never behave like that again.

Ted's mother finally grew very fond of Moira. She had only been afraid that their way of life was changing. At her funeral many years later, when she was eighty two years old, all her old friends who came back to the house after, said she had always spoken with great love and respect for her daughter-in-law.

Chapter 19

In the summer of 1934, Ambrose's band was engaged to appear at the Casino in Biarritz, on the South West Coast of France, next door to Spain.

On the journey to France, the sea was very rough. Ted had decided they would stay in the car on the boat deck of the ferry, thinking it would be comfortable with pillows and a small mattress for Moira if she got tired on the long drive south. What he hadn't realised was that the cars were fastened to the deck with chains. Every time the boat rolled, the cars rolled even more to the length of the chains. The petrol fumes were horrendous and Ted, who had never been a good sailor, was so sea sick he turned green and eventually Moira called a sailor over for help. He tied Ted to a chair on the open deck to get some fresh air, but Ted really felt like dying.

As you, dear reader, will realise, the ferries in those days were not the luxurious boats they are now.

The trip was to include two nights in Paris to make up for not having enjoyed a honeymoon. Ted had booked seats for the 'Follies Bergere', the very well known Parisian nude show. After his dreadful sea sickness he was not feeling too well, and although the show was beautifully presented, the theatre was very hot and by the interval, they both decided they had had enough, and went back to the hotel.

The rest of the journey was uneventful, until they reached Bordeaux. There was a very frightening thunderstorm overhead and suddenly they were stopped by men waving their arms frantically to hold them up. A huge tree had fallen right across the road, blocking the way. By the time they checked into a hotel in Bordeaux it was very late, they were very tired and did not notice that the bedroom was not too clean. The next morning they found that they had been bitten by bed bugs. The first and only time they had ever come in contact with the filthy little creatures.

They spent two months in Biarritz. During that time they decided they would like to visit Lourdes and see the Holy Grotto. They undertook the long drive through Pau, but when they got to Lourdes, a priest, on seeing that Moira was wearing slacks (trousers) for comfort told her that she could not enter the Grotto. Naturally, she was very upset but told Ted he could tell her all about it. He was really angry, even more so, when the priest tried to sell him picture postcards of it and he refused. They left, feeling sad and upset.

Ted decided to drive back to Biarritz a different way over the mountains. They started climbing, not realising that the mountain was very high and there was no turning back. The road was very rough and narrow with precipice drops at the side. When they got to the point where they saw no sign of habitation and only mountain sheep they began to feel very worried. On reaching the summit, it was one of the highest cols. in the Pyrenees, there was a sole building, which was a convalescent home for tuberculosis patients, and they had no alternative but to continue their journey down the very deep descent.

The first place they reached was a winter ski resort called 'Eaux Chaud'. On they went until reaching another small place called 'Eaux Bonne'. The sun was setting, a fabulous burning deep red, the sun roof of the car was open, and suddenly the car was filled by flying black beetles. Both of them were terrified, and got out of the car as swiftly as they could. The brakes were red hot, and Ted was afraid they would not be able to continue their journey. A petrol station luckily was nearby, and they managed to cool the brakes and tyres down and refuel.

By then, it was dark - there was no telephone to ring Biarritz and Ted knew he was not going to be able to get to work on time. What he did not know was the panic it caused the band and the hotel proprietor, who thought they had been involved in an accident. They eventually arrived at 1am much to everybody's relief.

Moira had said that if they had to climb another mountain, she was going to stay at Eaux Bonne and have her baby there! However, it all turned out well.

Chapter 20

Many nights, after the musicians had finished work at the casino about 4am, Ted and a couple of friends played snooker. On arriving back at the hotel about 5.30, he presented Moira with a beautiful fresh bread roll, coated in caviar, and a small bottle of Izarra, a liqueur made from the flowers of the Pyrenees, as a "please forgive me" gift. It amused Moira very much, as it was hardly what the doctors would have ordered for a pregnant lady, seven and a half months gone, as a suitable diet. She really enjoyed it all, and it did her no harm.

Towards the end of the engagement, Ambrose, who was a heavy gambler, had been playing the tables in the casino. Twice he ran out of money and could not pay the band's wages. He had to fly back to London both times, to raise the necessary funds.

Besides the Lourdes trip, they had another outing - the underground tunnels in the Pyrenees are very historic. Napoleon had hidden his army in them, and Moira and Ted thought they ought to see them. It proved a disaster. The tunnels got deeper and deeper and the holes leading one into another got smaller and smaller. Moira nearly had a fit when the guide who was leading them lifted his lamp and pointed just above their heads. Within inches there were dozens of bats. They both had a fear of bats forever after, and Moira still has a fear of tunnels.

Many days when the band were rehearsing, Moira would sit in the car outside the casino, watching the people go by. She was fascinated to see the Prince of Wales and Mrs. Simpson together on several occasions, long before the news of their love affair was made public. One day, Mrs Simpson's shoe came off and she called out 'Hey David come and help me' and the future King Edward VIII quietly went back, down on his knees and helped her put her shoe back on.

Chapter 21

On the way home, Ted and Moira set off, determined to get as far as possible the first day. On arrival at Poitiers, they saw the dreadful results of a bad accident. This upset Moira, who started having labour pains. Ted was very frightened, and drove into the middle of the town where a policeman was directing traffic. He pointed to Moira's tummy saying "Baby, Baby". The policeman understood, got on to the step of the car, waved all the traffic away and blowing his whistle directed them to the nearest hospital. This convent hospital was run by nuns who were kindness itself. They called a specialist who was on vacation in Poitiers, who turned out to examine Moira and saw her again at 6am in the morning. He told her, that if Ted drove very slowly, they might just get home before the baby was born, but it depended on the sea being very calm, and the pains stopping.

The nuns were delightful. They begged Moira to stay. They said they would make baby clothes, and look after her because Ted would have to go on ahead. One of them stayed up all night with her holding her hand. What a difference this loving caring attitude of the Catholic religion was, to the uncaring arrogance of that one priest at Lourdes.

Thankfully, the specialist gave them the go ahead and they reached home safely. Their baby, Martin, was born four days later, in October, a month early and was a joy and delight.

Grandma and Martin 1935

Chapter 22

Soon after Martin was born, Ambrose sacked Ted. It was a bitter blow after eight years in the job, a new house and a new baby. Ted felt his world was crumbling about him and his playing suffered. It turned out to be the best thing for him. He became a freelance and learned to stand on his own feet, instead of just turning up for a secure job. His confidence in himself grew, but he needed a regular income.

Sydney Lipton was the angel that came along. He offered Ted the trombone lead in his band at the Grosvenor House, deferred a lot to him on what he wanted to play, solos etc. and became a very dear friend.

Ted learned the rudiments of band leading and the responsibilities of it, and possibly the first seed was sewn, that he would like to have his own band. It was a very happy partnership for Ted, and his playing improved out of all recognition because of the faith Syd Lipton had in him.

The golf was enjoyable too. Ted was a very good golfer and keen. Syd, not so good but happy playing. One day, when playing golf at Richmond, they were chatting and talking 'shop' as they approached the green. Syd took a number two iron instead of a putter, took a full swing, and drove the ball out of sight, goodness knows where. They curled up laughing.

Marion Lipton (Syd's wife) and Moira became good friends and spent many evenings together while their husband's were working. One New Year's Eve, they were sitting alone at a table, drinking hock and watching all the other people having a good time, when Marion said 'Come on, let's go and sit near the band. At least we will be near them'. They sat on the edge of the stand. Before long, a young man approached them, swept Moira up in his arms and danced off with her. He asked her what she was doing alone, and she said 'My husband is the trombone player in the band'. As they danced in front of the band, the young man picked Moira up, and called to Ted 'Look what I've got!' Ted was not amused.

Syd and Marion had a lovely daughter called Celia, who had a very good singing voice. She now lives in America and is a famous society hostess.

Chapter 23

During that time in 1938, their daughter Valerie, now always called Val, was born. Ted was in seventh heaven. He had always wanted a daughter and now he had this sweet adorable little girl. He told Moira that for every daughter she gave him, he would give her a diamond ring. He gave her a diamond eternity ring for Val, which Val herself wears today with pride. She is also so like Ted. When she was eighteen months old, someone came up to Moira in Blackpool and said, "that must be Ted Heath's daughter". True - later in life, it is still said to her. Both in looks and nature, she is a chip off the old block. The only thing different, she herself says is that she hasn't a moustache, and does not play the trombone.

Ted stayed with Sydney Lipton right up to the outbreak of war. They were touring in Scotland, the news was dire, and Ted felt that Aberdeen, where they were playing, being a port on the North Sea, was a dangerous place to be in. He was afraid it might be one of the first places to be bombed from across the North Sea. The family, Moira, Ray, Bobby, Martin, Val and Lucy, a Welsh girl they employed to help look after the little ones, were all taken to a small place outside Aberdeen called Inch. The only rooms available were in the local pub. The three boys were in one bedroom, and Moira, Val and Lucy in the other. Ted left them with a heavy heart, to return to work in Aberdeen, knowing that war was now inevitable.

The pub was buzzing with people, with the 'drink and be merry, for tomorrow we may die' attitude, and Lucy, dear girl, finally slept across the door of their bedroom, to stop the drunks from bursting in.

The next day, Ted drove out to see if they were all right, and Moira said "Please take us away from here. Anything, including bombing is better than this", So they drove back to Aberdeen. On arriving there, they heard that Chamberlain, the Prime Minister had declared war on Germany. Every theatre, concert hall, and dance halls were shutting down, so the family drove on to Banchory, a beautiful place on the river Dee near Balmoral, where the Queen's castle is.

They stayed there a few days, but Ted was eager to find out what was going to happen, and decided to go back to Blackpool, leave the family among friends, and he would go to London. People were very welcoming and kind in Blackpool, and very willing to put them up, even though the town was crowded and full of expectant mothers, who had been evacuated there from Manchester and Liverpool, both potential bomb targets.

But the night before Ted was leaving for London, he and Moira clung together in each other's arms, she in tears, and they decided they could, and would face whatever lay ahead, together rather than be separated. The decision made, they all drove down to Wimbledon to face whatever fate held in store for them.

Bobby, Martin and Ray

Martin, Bobby, Ted, Ray and Val

46

Chapter 24

While they had been away in the north, Grandma, Uncle Porkie and Auntie Barbara had been looking after Oak Cottage.

Ted had had a deep air raid shelter built in the garden, at the time of the Munich Conference the year before. Unfortunately, it had been a bit neglected and water plus condensation had seeped in, so there was about a foot of water in it. There was a flat bottomed dinghy that the children had enjoyed using on holiday and the three old people put that down in the shelter and solemnly sat in it, with the water lapping around them, waiting for the bombs to fall.

Happily, it didn't happen then, but later, Wimbledon was a target for high explosive bombs and worse still, the flying bombs and the incredible bravery of Grandma and many other old people, was an inspiration to everybody.

Ted and Val

Chapter 25

At the beginning of the war, the entertainment business was at a standstill, until it began to be realised that London, especially, was not going to be immediately destroyed by bombs.

Places began opening again, and people started going to dinner dances as they had previously been used to doing. Ted was asked by Maurice Winnick to join his band at the Dorchester Hotel.

A short time afterwards, Geraldo who had a big and important band, with regular broadcasts offered Ted the job in the trombone section. This was to last throughout the duration of the war. Entertainment was considered to be of paramount importance in keeping up the morale of the people and the armed forces. Ted was too old to be called up for the army, and the Geraldo job was a national service. They played many, many broadcasts, dances and concerts, especially for the soldiers. They travelled to France, Holland, Belgium and the Middle East with E.N.S.A. of which later Geraldo was made a major.

When things began to become too dangerous in London, the B.B.C was evacuated to Bristol to broadcast from there. Ted decided that he wanted his family to be at least in the same half of England as he was, rather than in London, in case there was the threatened invasion by the Germans.

He rented the bungalow, they had rented in the past for summer holidays at Bigbury-on-Sea in South Devon and the family, plus Lucy moved in.

The comical thing is that one of the first bombs of the war was dropped by a German plane from a reconnaissance raid on Plymouth, on Modbury, the next village to Bigbury. Fortunately, there was little damage done.

The house was situated on the cliff top, with a sheer drop to the beach from the bottom of the garden. One night, when the moon was at its brightest and full, Moira and Lucy were listening to Geraldo's band (Ted among them) broadcasting from Bristol. The children were in bed.

It was such a beautiful night, they were sitting with the French windows open, and the curtains undrawn, when suddenly Moira saw, coming up the garden edge from the cliff, a silhouette of a tin hat and a gun. Her heart went cold, she thought this must be the beginning of the long expected invasion. She said to Lucy, "Get the children very, very quietly into the corridor, impress on them they must be absolutely silent" and she went out to face the German Army. Her relief was unimaginable when it turned out to be their landlord, a member of the Home Guard, who knew of a small path at the top of the cliff, and was checking that all was well.

From then on, it was agreed that he should whistle "Run Rabbit, Run" a very popular song at that time, so that she would know that it was him.

**Jack Collier, Maurice Burman and Ted, with Geraldo's band
on way to Middle East. ENSA**

Chapter 26

With the 'phoney war' as it was known continuing, things were returning to normal in London, and Geraldo's band went back to broadcasting from London. The family moved back home to Oak Cottage.

Petrol was getting very short, and before it was totally forbidden to use a car for personal reasons, Ted decided that paraffin might be a good substitute. He had a big old Buick, which fantastically did run on paraffin, but not for long. The smoke and smell were unbelievable, and to start it, the stronger members of the family, Ray, Bobby and Moira, and any handy neighbours would push it down the hill to start the engine. A strange sight! But what a car

Ted also decided that they would have a swimming pool, so they started digging a hole in the garden. They bricked it and cemented it, and filled it with the garden hose. But his calculations were a little awry. There was no way to empty it, other than a very small electric pump and flood the garden. Help, however, was at hand. The Fire Brigade was keen to have it, as an emergency water supply, to put out fires from incendiary bombs. In return for a crate of beer, they emptied it and refilled it regularly so the children could learn to swim.

As previously mentioned, Ted had the foresight to build a deep air raid shelter in the garden. The safety of his family was of deep concern to him.

Some neighbours at that time before the war, thought he was being a 'scary cat', but his vision and care proved to them all that he was right.

On the first day of an aerial dog fight over Wimbledon, they sheltered twenty small children with their mothers, plus his own family in the shelter. A gramophone playing loudly to drown the sounds of the shooting overhead.

The shelter became a necessity for the children to be safe as they slept. It was arranged that there were four bunk beds for the children, Ray, Bobby, Martin and Val, and two deck chairs facing each other, with a pouffe (foot stool) in between for Ted's mother and Moira. They underwent some very heavy bombing from high explosive bombs. The house opposite was demolished, but luckily the people had gone into the country for the night for safety. As the bombs got nearer and nearer, in 'sticks' of seven, Grandma would very quietly start to do up her corsets (she would never take them off completely) and if she was going to die, she would be properly dressed. After the air raid was over, and the all clear had sounded, Moira produced a treasured bottle of the liqueur Benedictine, and she and Ted's mother had a small taste. As the raids continued, the precious drink got smaller and smaller, and finished up as just a sip. It is likely that the Benedictine monks who made the liqueur would not have dreamed that their elixir would have given two ladies so much comfort in the aftermath of danger in a shelter underground in a garden in Wimbledon.

One night, when unusually Ted was home, Moira decided that she could not bear to sleep underground like an animal, and that she wanted to sleep in Ted's arms in their own bed. It was fine at first, and then the air raid sirens sounded. Simultaneously, the sound of a German bomber (a distinctive sound) approaching nearer and nearer, and lower and lower, turned Ted and Moira to stone. She felt that it was her fault and her selfish desire to be with Ted upstairs, that they were going to die, and leave their children orphans. There was suddenly an enormous flash and explosion. The room was lit up, even through the blackout curtains. Then the noise of the fire engines and ambulance. The German pilot had been looking for a place to land, away from houses, and had crashed on Royal Wimbledon Golf Course a short distance from Oak Cottage. Bobby, who knew no fear, came out of the air raid shelter at dawn and rushed to the scene. He returned home a short time later, with his eyes on stalks and very excited. He related his horribly gruesome story of seeing German brains on a stone post, and a foot, without a boot, lying on the ground. He wanted to pick it up and take it home but was firmly stopped by the police, and sent packing. His comment was "It was a perfect foot, it didn't even have a corn". Such is the resilience of innocent childhood that the horrors of war could not destroy.

To continue this theme, later on, after a daylight raid on Raynes Park, a German plane crashed in flames. Bobby got on his bicycle, raced to the scene, and when he finally got home, the excitement of it overcame the awfulness of the scene, and he said, "The smell of German flesh was lovely. Like Sunday dinner!" Ugh!

Chapter 27

To show Ted's concern for his family, he purchased some rabbits and chickens, so at least they would not starve. The first rabbit grew and grew, and naturally became a family pet called 'Moses' (for no particular reason). When the time came for Moses to be eaten, before he became too tough, there was an outcry "We would sooner starve - we will never eat rabbit again", from the whole family, and that was that. The rabbits were given to the milkman, except for one. From then on, every 'rabbit pie' was believed to be a chicken pie, and eaten with relish

Ted played with the band that accompanied the Ben Lyon and Bebe Daniels Show. "Hi, Gang" with Vic Oliver, at the Paris Cinema. They became friends and when the rabbits were being given away, Ted gave Bebe one for a pet. There is no record of whether the little thing lived a life of luxury or suffered eventually the same fate as Moses.

The chickens were a great success and provided unlimited eggs, which were bartered with neighbours and friends for tinned food, sugar and other rationed luxuries.

A more serious episode was while they were doing the show from the Paris cinema, the Cafe de Paris was bombed. A direct hit, the bomb went through the glass dome roof, although the Cafe was considered safely underground. Many people were killed, mostly by the blast, as they danced or sat at their tables, among them the bandleader, Snake Hips Johnson and the bass player. The musicians from the Paris, on hearing of this dreadful tragedy, all rushed to the scene, Ted with them, hoping they could help. It was a disaster that was to remain in Ted's heart for a long, long time.

Chapter 28

Then came the time when the Geraldo Band were booked to go to the Middle East with E.N.S.A. The dreaded day was October 13th, Moira's birthday. They both felt they were saying 'Goodbye' for ever particularly as Ted suffered terribly from sea sickness (remember their voyage to France) and it was the time of the equinoctial gales. Moira was afraid that Ted would be so ill that if a submarine torpedoed them, he would not try to save himself. He would gladly drown. Imagine her relief, when six weeks later she received his first letter home, from Gibraltar. It was full of "how lovely the grub was. The bread was white and like cake" and so on in that vein. Ted was cured of his sea sickness for the rest of his life.

The band went to Alexandria where there were peacocks in the garden of the hotel, and then through the desert, entertaining the troops. Very welcome, and giving them much needed morale building. As the convoy was driving through the desert, a soldier in an army truck called out "Don't forget to play That Lovely Weekend" tonight - Ted was thrilled to think that his song was as popular as that.

That tour ended in Cairo. The fleshpots and the good life after the hardships of desert travelling and unending sand, was enjoyable. They stayed at the British Club at Gezira, which was very luxurious and beautiful.

When the time came to go home, they were all longing to be with their wives and families. Geraldo had promised they would be home for Christmas, but no arrangements had been made for transport. Geraldo, his brother Syd Bright, the pianist and Dorothy Carless the vocalist, flew home, leaving the musicians virtually stranded with no money. They had been earning only eight pounds a week, some of which was kept at home on expenses there. As there was no one to fix things, they voted Ted as their spokesman, and trusted him to get them home. The only thing he could think of doing was to go and see Sarah Churchill, whom he had met with Vic Oliver, her husband, on the "Hi Gang Show". She had accompanied her father, the great Winston Churchill to Cairo for the Cairo Conference. Although Churchill was already beginning to feel unwell with the pneumonia he was later to suffer, the great man spoke to General Ismay about getting the musicians back to England. It was arranged, strictly against military and naval security to accommodate the band on the frigate H.M.S. London.

They slept in hammocks slung over the Petty Officers mess, and H.M.S. London made its way to Gibraltar to await Churchill there. He was due to sail home on the King George V, a huge ship. His illness held the whole convoy up, and as the musicians were unofficially aboard the London, officially they didn't exist and they could not go ashore. To pass the time, Ted arranged to play concerts on board the British ships in harbour. Another experience to encourage him, eventually to lead his own band.

These concerts went down very well, so much so, that years later in peacetime, H.M.S. King George V was moored off Blackpool and the sailors went to the Empire Ballroom to hear Ted's band. One of the sailors gave Ted's daughter Val, the ribbon from his hat, as a remembrance of the concert in Gibraltar Harbour.

The following day, the band were all invited plus wives and children to go aboard. A tender was sent for them, but when they got to the enormous ship, the swell was fifteen feet. Paul Carpenter was the first to jump the frightening gap. Val, who like her father before her, was very sea sick, was swung over by Johnny Gray and a sailor and Johnny then jumped. The Commander then said it was too dangerous for any more, and they had to turn back to shore.

Ted, Moira and Martin spent anxious hours worrying about Val, and what was happening. When she, with Paul and Johnny finally returned that evening, she had a story to tell. She was immediately over her sea sickness like being on a huge building rather than a ship, and was shown all over the ship, including the bridge and gun sites, a great honour. They were wined and dined (in Val's case orange juice) and had a wonderful time. They returned in sailors' waterproofs and sou'westers. Val's pockets were full of sweets and chewing gum - a wonderful experience. Martin was, needless to say, very envious of his sister.

To revert to the Middle East tour, the convoy with H.M.S. London finally sailed from Gibraltar for home. They arrived at a secret destination, later revealed as Greenock in Scotland the night before Christmas Eve. Ted had to arrange a van in London to transport the instruments of the musicians, so he telephoned Moira, unable for security reasons to say where they were, and asked her to have a van waiting at Euston station in some seven hours time and that it would be nice if she were there too. This was wonderful news. She arranged the van and herself went to Euston to wait. There was no knowing what time the train would arrive, or what platform it would be at, so it was a question of watching and waiting, not daring even to have a coffee in case the train came in then. The wait was somewhat extended, from midnight to eleven o'clock next morning, Christmas Eve.

At last the 'ghost train' arrived, with hundreds of sailors on board, coming home on leave, and the musicians. They were right at the back end of the train, and Moira was vainly endeavouring to get through to them, when a big burly sailor said, "Where are you trying to get to, lady?" Moira replied "My husband is Ted Heath, with the musicians". The sailor put his arms out, shouted "make way for the little lady" and she had a passage made for her. When Ted saw her, his face was beaming, his cup was full.

That homecoming was a joyous one. Ted had brought all sorts of goodies from Cairo, including a gold charm for Val, of an Egyptian slipper. In the excitement of unwrapping everything and the general chaos, the little charm was thrown with wrapping paper into the kitchen boiler and melted, much to Val's distress. However, there was a consolation because Ted had also bought her a little doll, which became a great favourite.

He had also brought, safely, an Egyptian leather holdall, full of liquers, Green Chartreuse, Kummel, Benedictine and Grand Marnier. He put it down on the kitchen floor, and a couple of the bottles broke, and the kitchen reeked of the beautiful smell of Grand Marnier and Kummel running all over the floor. They didn't know whether to laugh or cry. He had safely carried them all that distance only to break them at home!

On another trip he had bought a beautiful Sevres lamp and hand painted shade. This survived the many journeys home, including crossing France and Belgium, hung from the roof of the truck they travelled in.

Chapter 29

Before Geraldo's band left for the Middle East, Ted and Moira had been listening to the current 'pop' songs. Moira said "I'm sure we can write something better than this rubbish". She suggested that a poem she had written for Ted just before the war, as a thank you for a very rare weekend break in Hastings, and placed on his pillow, would make, with a few alterations, a good wartime song. Ted agreed, and he wrote the music for the updated lyric. He composed the music, playing it on his trombone.

When Geraldo was doing a series of broadcasts, he came up with the idea of playing each week, a personal choice of the musicians. When it came to Ted's turn, Ted asked for his and Moira's song (which had been turned down by several music publishers). It was called 'I Haven't Said Thanks for that Lovely Weekend'. Geraldo wasn't that keen, but said if Ted paid for the arrangement himself, he would do it. This was done, and Dorothy Carless sang it on the broadcast. It was an instant hit. Dorothy sang it beautifully and with great feeling. The next few days, letters poured in from people saying it described their last few days before their loved ones went overseas, and brought back many happy memories.

Bradbury Wood, music publishers of renown telephoned and immediately agreed to publish it. It became a huge hit.

While Ted was away in the Middle East, every day there were several different renderings of 'Lovely Weekend'. It became a normal occurrence in Oak Cottage for the radio to be on, Moira upstairs, probably in the bath! when once more some band was playing their song. The children would be shouting "Mummy, they are playing Lovely Weekend again". It was in the top twenty for twenty six weeks.

A wonderful outcome of the success of the song, were the royalties. That heaven-sent windfall, eventually helped Ted to start his own band, and pay for the arrangements and musicians.

That Lovely Weekend

Verse

Darling – Here's my letter, I'm writing through my tears
A few sweet words to thank you for lovely souvenirs
Memories you gave me still echo in my heart
I'll dream of them, while we're apart

Chorus

I haven't said thanks for that lovely weekend

Those two days of heaven you helped me to spend,
The thrill of your kiss as you stepped off the train,
The smile in your eyes, like the sun after rain.
To mark the occasion, we went out to dine,
Remember the laughter, the music, the wine?
The drive in the taxi, when midnight had flown,
Then breakfast next morning, just we two alone!
You had to go, the time was so short, we both had so much to say
Your kit to be packed, the train to be caught,
Sorry I cried, but I just felt that way.
And now you have gone dear, this letter I pen,
My heart travels with you, 'till we meet again
Keep smiling my darling, and one day we'll spend
A lifetime as sweet as that Lovely Weekend.

Chapter 30

At the end of the war, Moira wrote another lyric entitled "I'm Gonna Love that Guy" and Ted put the music to it. That also was a great hit, especially so in the United States. A G.I. had heard it in England, took it home to New York, and told a music publisher there that he had found a great song. It too, was a success. Among many versions was that of Perry Como, which sold a million copies. Betty Grable featured it in a seven minute spot in a film called "Call me Mister".

I'm Gonna Love That Guy

Verse
I've made out a list of the things that I've missed and wanted to do
And right at the head, in letters of red, is the first of the few
This promise I've made, cross my heart, hope to die,
Is the first of the first for my honey and I.

Chorus
I'm gonna love that guy like he's never been loved before
I'm gonna show that guy he's the fella that I adore
When he's in my arms tonight, our dreams will all come true
Gonna hold him closely ever so tight, all of my whole life through
I'm gonna kiss that guy like he's never been kissed before
And though I miss that guy, it'll be worth the waiting for,
We'll never part again, he'll hold my heart again for ever and ever more
I'm gonna love that guy like he's never never ever been loved before.

The success of 'I'm Gonna Love that Guy' in America made up for the disappointment that 'Lovely Weekend' was banned there earlier in the war, as being suggestive! Moira offered to alter the lyric, to make it obvious that the couple were married. It had never entered her head that they were not, but was told that even the title was suggestive. Gracie Fields, who was giving concerts in the States, sang it at every one, to great applause, but was forbidden to broadcast it - one cannot imagine what they would think of present day lyrics.

My Dear Ted Heath and Mrs Ted,

Thank you for your nice letter, well your song is the favourite one with me. I love singing it and was very disappointed when they wouldn't let me broadcast it in New York. To this day they wouldn't pass it, said it was about two unmarried people. Daft B-------- who ever is in charge of censorship, never mind I'll do it yet. I start my own broadcast programme in October, 5 days a week Monday to Friday, one song every day and I'll scrap to do Lovely Weekend. Send me any more you have also any good stories, as I'm supposed to sing one song and tell a gag.

Well Good Luck to you both,

Yours very sincerely,

Gracie Fields

The royalties from 'I'm Gonna Love That Guy' and 'Lovely Weekend' helped considerably for Ted to be able to continue keeping the band together, more of which later.

Chapter 31

After a short period of quiet on the bombing front, the wonderful Battle of Britain's young airmen had seen off, with great courage, but considerable loss of life, the German onslaught from their air force, the Luftwaffe but then a new menace started.

One night, a huge explosion occurred, heard for miles, and the rumour went around that a gasometer in Chiswick had exploded, that was not so. It was the beginning of the most terrifying bombing that England had ever experienced. The bombs were small pilotless planes, later known as V.1's (nicknamed doodlebugs) that dived at pre-chosen targets, and were capable of doing enormous blast damage, and very destructive to the morale of the people.

One target that had been chosen was the hideaway place of General Eisenhower, the American Commander in Chief - a house called "Telegraph Cottage" in Coombe Hill, near Kingston on Thames. The route the flying bombs took, were over Wimbledon and the Heath's reckoned their large Oak tree was the pointer.

The raids were practically continuous, the alerts eventually lasting twenty-four hours and life once again had to be adjusted to air raid shelter living for the children. All meals were eaten in the shelter in the garden so that they could be eaten without interruption and in safety. Every night, bedtime was normal, but down underground. Martin's headmistress from the Wimbledon Common Preparatory School, nicknamed 'The Squirrels,' bicycled from her home every morning and continued his lessons in the shelter - a wonderful lady.

During the day, ears were constantly on the alert, to listen for the approach of the V.1's. While the sound of the engine was audible, it was safe, but as soon as the engine cut out, the bomb either dropped immediately, or glided for an unknown time and distance silently, before dropping and detonating, causing immense destruction, principally from blast.

During the daytime, if there was enough time, Moira hustled the children, Grandma and Lucy, down to the shelter. But sometimes there was no time, and they huddled in the cupboard under the stairs, believing it was the safest place to be - Lucy said her prayers in Welsh and they were all frightened.

One day, the damage around Oak Cottage was considerable. A house on Copse Hill, just down the road was a direct hit, and the people in it were killed, and another house in a road adjoining Copse Hill, Hood Road off Barham Road was also demolished.

The tiles, on the roof of Oak Cottage, were blown off, and the windows which were leaded lights, were blown out and had to be covered with brown paper, to keep out the rain. After one particularly bad raid, the alert still on, Grandma and Moira went up from the shelter to the house, to see what further damage had been done. The drawing room floor was covered in soot from the chimney – inches thick on the carpet. They set to, to clean up the mess, and with their faces black from soot, were busy when they heard a cheery voice calling out "Is there anybody alive there?" It was Debroy Somers, a famous bandleader, who lived up Barham Road, a short distance from Oak Cottage. He offered the family sanctuary in his house for as long as they wanted. They were extremely grateful but declined, feeling the shelter offered them greater safety.

When Ted returned home from broadcasting that night, he was horrified at the damage, and decided that the family must go to a place of safety. They had previously stayed before the war, in a lovely little place in Cornwall called Trebetherick and he telephoned the one and only hotel there, and booked a room for Moira and the two small children. Grandma, Bobby and Ray had opted to stay on in Wimbledon.

The little ones were showing signs of fear, every time they heard an aircraft and it was essential to get them away.

Incidentally, Carroll Gibbons, the very famous bandleader at the Savoy Hotel London had a house down there.

Chapter 32

They stayed there for three weeks, then the hotel was fully booked. The owner of the hotel was prepared to let them stay, and have all their meals and to spend the days there, and if necessary to provide them with beds and bedding, if they could find somewhere to sleep. There was a house opposite the hotel which had an empty clean garage, which would have been ideal for the little family to sleep in, but the owners said they might need the garage for storing luggage and boxes. They refused all offers of money and had no sympathy for their plight. Talk about ' no room at the inn' - Moira told them they should have to spend time in London and see how people were suffering from the flying bombs. They didn't really know there was a war on, butter and meat rationing was virtually ignored, their minds and hearts were closed.

Ted firmly refused to let them return home to the dangers, so Moira, Martin and Val went round from house to house seeking accommodation. The local evacuation officer could not help. Everyone who could and would take in evacuees were full up including Carroll Gibbons.

On one of their treks, they were walking across St. Enodoc golf course (famous for John Betjamin's poem about the tiny church), Martin was piggybacking Val, when they met a lady walking there. She was muffled up, in a long skirt, jacket and large hat with a white veil covering her face, which was thickly covered with white face powder. She spoke to them, and wanted to know about them. Moira told her they were trying to find somewhere to stay, but having no luck. She instantly said they could stay in her house for as long as they needed. The only snag was that her house was in Plymouth, which was just as badly bombed as London. This dear lady was Lady Asquith, who was then Member of Parliament for Plymouth. A kind and generous hearted woman.

Finally, a lovely family, who had rented a house in Trebetherick there much earlier and with whom they had made friends on the beach, offered to make room for the tired and pathetic little family. They put their children, three of them in one room, and gave the Heaths a bedroom. Their name was Cook, of the Donald Cook tinned meat people. For a time, Moira and the children ate all their meals at the hotel, but the weather became appalling.

It was a mile walk from the house, across a field, and the children had bad coughs. Mrs. Cook finally could not bear to see Moira and the children struggling every day to eat at the hotel, and suggested they collected their ration books and live en famille with them. Their kindness will never be forgotten. A much needed good turn to restore Moira's faith in human nature, after the selfishness of some of the local people. Despite this one unhappy memory, the tradition of Trebetherick lasts with Ted and Moira's children, grandchildren and great grandchildren who spend holidays there to this day.

Chapter 33

When there had been a time of cessation of the bombings, Ted decided they could return home. The look of strain on Grandma's face was evident, and Moira thought her ears had grown bigger, through listening for the engines of the V1's. At least their sense of humour was surviving. Geraldo had booked a tour of Scotland with his band and Ted decided to take his family with him. The day before they left for Scotland there was an unbelievable explosion in Tottenham Court Road, London. Nobody had heard any sound of approaching aircraft or bombs, but the damage and destruction was horrific. Plate glass windows from the shops had blown out and the broken glass had cut poor people to pieces. This was the beginning of the V2's more devastating than the V1's in the damage they did, and just as frightening, because the sound of their approach and exploding was heard after it happened.

Ted was very relieved to get the family away.

The first hotel they stayed in, in Scotland was the Midland in Glasgow. Very comfortable and old fashioned. The beds were brass knobbed, and Ted would unscrew the ends and hide them in the children's beds, much to their delight and laughter. After Glasgow they moved on to Edinburgh. A most welcome relief from the endless air raid alerts in London. Most of Geraldo's musicians had their wives with them, including Geraldo.

As the war continued, and the Americans were playing a larger and larger part, in helping the allies in conquering Germany, the Americans were spending their leaves in London. The ever-growing contingents of U.S. troops were stationed around England. American entertainers were flying over to entertain their men. Bing Crosby, Bob Hope and many others, too numerous to mention, and most importantly to British musicians, Glenn Miller and the US Air Force Band. Ted managed to hear this wonderful band at the Queensbury Club and in some aircraft hangers around London. He persuaded Glenn to bring his band to the London Coliseum for the Jazz Jamboree in aid of the musicians Benevolent Fund, which, as can be imagined was a huge success. Glenn and Ted got on very well together 'like to like', and Glenn was very encouraging to Ted about starting his own band. He said he would like to exchange arrangements with Ted, when he returned to the States, and would leave Ted his trombone. Sadly, as history records, he was never to return from his ill fated flight to France, but he left a never to be forgotten memory of his music to the world, and to Ted, a cherished memory of a fine musician and leader, an inspiration and friend.

Chapter 34

During the latter part of the war, Ted's desire to have his own band was becoming an obsession. After long discussions with Moira (should he, shouldn't he?), they decided that it was do or die. Moira realised that if he didn't do it, he would regret it for the rest of his life, and Ted thought he would probably finish up as a pit musician in the Chiswick Empire Orchestra, a dreadful fate for a brilliant musician. Not that there was anything wrong with the Chiswick Empire, it was just a typical variety theatre, but death to the ambitions and aspirations of a musician like Ted. The decision meant that they were going to risk their whole security, on the enormous gamble, but the dream was so strong, there was no denying it.

Ted made plans to try and get some broadcasts. Gather the musicians he wanted from all over the place, and start building up the Ted Heath Band. He was unable to leave his job with Geraldo because entertainment was considered of such national importance for the morale of the people and the forces, that it was a protected job. However, he did manage to get some broadcasts and overseas transcriptions, especially thanks to Pat Dixon of the BBC

Amongst the musicians, and to this day, a highly valued and important member of the band was Kenny Baker, who was serving in the Royal Air Force. Ted used all his powers of persuasion to get the various commanding officers to allow their men to go to London to do the broadcasts. This was usually given, when at all possible. However, on one occasion, Kenny had not been given leave. He sneaked away from the camp, hid his uniform somewhere near the station, boarded a train for London, did the broadcast, and returned without being found out. Kenny was one of the most important and loyal members of Ted's band for many years.

Ted, naturally at the beginning, was using some of his friends in the band. They were familiar buddies, and were not prepared to be disciplined by their old pal. On one broadcast, Max Goldberg, a top trumpet player was doing a crossword puzzle, while the band were playing. Ted was furious and decided there and then that old friendships did not make for the building up of the kind of band he wanted. His musicians must respect and defer to him as leader, not 'chum'. This caused him and them some distress, but the somewhat lonely life of a bandleader was the only way. He lost some of his friends, including George Smith who had been his best man at his and Moira's wedding and was Val's godfather, because of this -- but it was never to be easy.

Ted and Moira

Martin, Nick, Moira, Tim, Val and Ted with ivory tusk brought from Africa by Moira's grandfather

Ted Heath and his Music

Chapter 35

Meanwhile, the sound of Ted Heath and his music was becoming an established fact, although still in its infancy.

On V.E. Day, when the war in Europe was officially over, Ted gave in his notice to Geraldo, and told him he was going to have his own band. Gerry said he was mad, and that "he would lose his shirt" but there was no holding back. He was totally committed and determined that this was the road he must take.

The musicians he chose and wanted for his band were all brilliant, dedicated men. Only the best was good enough, among them of course Jack Parnell, a founder member, Ted had always said, "when I have my own band, my musicians will not have to walk through the back door and the kitchens to work. They will walk through the front door and be treated like the talented gentlemen they are. They will also only stay in good hotels on tour, not dreary digs, and travel in comfort".

Times were very hard. The recession after the war had left people hard up. There was considerable unemployment, men demobbed from the forces were unable to get work, and Ted found it extremely difficult to keep the band going. On top of this, a meeting of some of the established bandleaders had met, Ambrose among them, and decided with the BBC that a band could not have broadcasts, unless they were fully employed full time, by a band leader, and not gathered together for single broadcasts. This was to the advantage of the leaders, who had bands resident at the big hotels and aimed at 'that upstart Ted Heath', and knocking him off the map. This was not a situation that Ted would give in to. He formed his regular band and struggled to keep his head above water. On one occasion, they were playing in Manchester. The takings were not even enough to pay the train fares, let alone the musicians' salaries. They appointed Jack Parnell to speak to Ted on the train home, and said they would forego their money. They wanted to save the band, and keep it going, because they were playing the sort of music and arrangements they loved and wanted to be a part of it. This gesture was so wonderful, Ted was forever grateful. Though times were so hard, Ted's enthusiasm and love of the band never faltered. After one gig they played he came home and said to Moira "the band was terrific, they played like angels - I had to give them another couple of quid to show my appreciation". That couple of quid for seventeen musicians was Moira's housekeeping money for the week! But they managed not to starve.

Chapter 36

During this time, the Band was touring all over Britain, working every night in a different town. It was hard, gruelling work, but their enthusiasm never faltered. Ted, eventually decided that he should buy a 'bus', fitted with comfortable reclining seats, a 'loo' and facilities for making tea and coffee, to save the musicians from having to drive enormous distances in their own cars. He himself loved driving and always drove to the venues but after a time the novelty of the 'bus' and the wages of the driver, no longer were viable, so it was discontinued.

Meanwhile, the fame of the band was spreading worldwide. They were invited to appear in Scandinavia where they were a huge success, both professionally and socially. It was decided that Moira would accompany Ted on this thrilling tour, and she was looking forward to it. A few days before they were due to leave, Martin was unwell. Moira called in the family doctor, Sam Rose, who at first sight thought it was flu - just as he was about to leave, Moira said "would you look at Martin's knee. He had a kick on it while playing rugby football at school, and it is causing him a lot of pain". Dr. Rose said, "thank God, you've told me. It could be osteomyelitis, or otherwise rheumatic fever. I am going to get him into hospital immediately and I'm going to inject him full of a new drug, an antibiotic called 'Penicillin' just released for civilian use". An ambulance (a Rolls Royce) was called and Martin was rushed to Wimbledon Cottage Hospital, just up the road from Oak Cottage. The specialist, who examined Martin, confirmed Dr. Rose's diagnosis, that it was osteomyelitis, and poor little Martin was given injections of penicillin every hour. At that time, the injection needles were huge and the penicillin was thick and viscous. The injections were horrendously painful but the skill of a local general practitioner and the intuition of a mother not only saved Martin's life but also his future health.

Before penicillin, fifty per cent of children died from the infection of the marrow of the bone and fifty per cent were crippled and had to have regular operations to scrape the marrow of the bone to prevent further infection. The family doctor was worth his weight in gold and told Moira that he would never let anything hurt her family. Where are the family doctors now? Martin was on the danger list for five weeks but recovered fully, thanks to Dr. Rose.

Chapter 37

Meanwhile, Ted had left with the band for Denmark, but obviously was worried and upset about Martin's illness.

During the Scandinavian tour the organisers had booked the bridal suite, filled with flowers for Moira and Ted. Among them was Jacques Kluger, who became a great friend during this time, and he and Ted later became partners in a publishing business 'Good Music'. They published several of Ted's original band numbers, and proved quite successful. Jack Heath, (no relation) was also an invaluable part of the company

At one of the concerts in Copenhagen, the hospitality, as always, was great. This particular night was no different. During the interval, Ted was plied with Aquavit, a virulent strong drink. Ted, who was not a drinker, could not take it and when he came back on stage for the second half of the show, he had to walk down a flight of stairs. He missed his footing, fell headlong taking the music stands of the sax section with him, and he was so embarrassed, he was on hands and knees picking up the music and putting it back on the stands. Everybody was very understanding but highly amused and the show went on, if anything to a more enthusiastic and exciting reception.

Incidentally, Ted was told during the tour that if a toast was drunk to someone, it was only good manners to drink a toast back - hence, leading literally to Ted's 'downfall'. Ted totally believed this advice, and followed it to the letter!

The whole tour was highly successful. Denmark, Norway and Sweden and a big fillip to the band. When they returned however, Moira, who met them at Liverpool Street Station said she had never seen such a bunch of the 'morning after the night before' reprobates in her life. Beside the musical side of the tour, the social side had been a roaring success. Perhaps too much so, in some cases. One member of the band (no names!) worrying how he was going to explain the love bites he had sustained to his wife.

One, not so amusing incident, at least to Ted, was when they were travelling between Sweden and Norway on the train. Ted, who had collected the takings in quite a considerable amount of cash, got worried about the customs at the border. So he hid the money under the carpet of the compartment on the train, thinking that that was a sensible thing to do. It was not so!! To his horror, when they came to the border, the train stopped and everybody was told to get out, they were changing trains! Ted, in a panic, scrabbled around, collecting the money, and stuffing it in his pockets, down his trousers, everywhere he could. Hot, bothered and red-faced, he must have looked anything but a smooth cool bandleader, casually going through the customs, in his beloved special 'camel' coat, which he proudly thought of as the smart garb for such a man. He really was a naïve innocent, but at least, he got through with the takings intact.

Later in Ted's career, he and Eddie Jones, a leading promoter, who became a great friend, and Tim's godfather, would count the money after a concert or dance, sitting on the couch in the drawing room at Oakfield. It was all in £1 notes and ten shilling notes, saying 'One for you, one for me'. There was a most unusual rapport and trust between them.

Chapter 38

It was Christmas time and Martin went home on crutches but he was soon recovering his health and strength and suffered no lasting effects.

It was a very special Christmas, although there was still rationing. The children were given bicycles, and the presents were put into sacks and left tumbling open by a Father Christmas who left a note to say "sorry, in a hurry". Ted would often pretend he had forgotten Christmas and there would be no presents. Then when the morning came, and the Christmas Tree was lit-up – there – hanging among the baubles, was a beautiful piece of jewellery for Moira and one year a white £5 note for Val.

Chapter 39

The band was gaining recognition and success all the time. They were broadcasting and were asked by the B.B.C to play 'Music While you Work'. Ted had an arrangement of the signature tune done, a jazzy version, which did not go down too well with the stuffed shirts! He also, at one time, had an arrangement with lovely harmonies of God Save the Queen, which was different, but he was politely asked not to use it.

The next summer after the Scandinavian tour, Ted and Moira retraced the band's footsteps, to show Moira the beautiful countries, and the charming people Ted had met, and Moira had missed because of Martin's illness.

They were driving Moira's first new car, a Hillman Minx convertible, bought from her share of the royalties of 'I'm Gonna Love that Guy'. Ted loved the little car, but was not so happy, when they were in the middle of Stockholm, the car stalled on a hill, the anti-thief lock Moira had had installed, automatically locked itself. Anything mechanical was totally beyond Ted's understanding, and to his embarrassment, they caused a huge traffic jam, and were completely helpless until they were towed to a garage to have major surgery done on the car, and the offending modern, wonder lock was removed. He soon recovered his equilibrium and sense of humour, and still enjoyed driving the pretty little blue car, on their special vacation. They went first to Copenhagen and were entertained by Jaques Kluger and his wife. Although there was still a shortage of food in Denmark, the Klugers produced a wonderful meal. Ted was very touched and was speechless, so Moira made a little 'thank you' speech, in which she especially thanked Mrs Kluger and said she must have made love to their butcher to get such a beautiful piece of steak! It concluded with kisses all round.

In Stockholm, they were entertained by the Decca representative and taken to a big boxing match. An American against a Swede. It was wonderful to see brain over brawn. The Swede was a teacher and retained his cool throughout the fight. The American was wild and unfit, and thoroughly outfought. It was not exactly Ted and Moira's cup of tea, but quite an experience and they enjoyed the delight of the Swedes at their man's victory.

Interestingly, throughout their trip, they were plied with rich foods, which they had become unused to during the war years of rationing. The full cream milk, especially, was tempting. There was always a jug on the table at every meal. They enjoyed the drinks of milk, much more than the Aquavit, but suffered upset liver attacks, having been more used to dried milk for so many years at home.

On the way home, having driven through Denmark, Sweden and Norway, they arrived late in the evening at the hotel in Gothenburg where they were to spend the night, before catching the boat back to England. When they arrived, the arrogant, pompous little manager, was very rude and told them there was no room booked for them. Ted was furious, and telling Moira to wait in the lobby of the hotel, went to telephone Stockholm to confirm that their room had been reserved. While Moira was sitting waiting patiently, the manager strutted up to her, like a little turkey cock, and shouted at her "Heath, Heath, your car is in the way. Remove it instantly". Everybody turned to look at Moira, who was astounded. She stood up very slowly and said "Do not speak to me like that, my man. I am British and we do not accept being treated with such bad manners". Everybody around applauded her and the little turkey cock subsided like a burst balloon. He then told her that there was a room for her and Ted, bowing and scraping he showed them to the best room in the hotel.

When they arrived back at Tilbury, the boat was two hours late docking. Ted had an engagement in Manchester and there was no chance of him being there on time, unless he flew. He told Moira to see to the luggage through the customs, while he saw the car through. All was well, and off they rushed for Ted to catch a plane. However, when Moira got home, she realised they had left one of their suitcases behind at Tilbury. It meant that she would have to travel down to Tilbury on the train to claim it personally. It was a miserable journey, several stops and changes. There was only one other passenger doing the same trip. Naturally, they got into conversation and she told him about why she was having to go to the customs to claim the case. When she went to the customs shed, who should she find but her travelling companion, who was the customs officer!

On the way back to London, he told her he was afraid she was going to tell him that they had smuggled things - nylons - perfume etc., but of course they had not, and he and she had a good laugh over the whole experience.

Meanwhile, although the band was becoming more and more popular, the costs of running it far outweighed the takings, and Ted was continually in debt, and desperately trying to keep the band going. His offices at 23 Albermarle Street were luxurious but expensive. Sharing with George Melachrino and Eric Robinson helped, but he was living on a knife's edge.

Help, however, was at hand. Tutti Camarata a very famous American leader, trumpet player and composer, came over from the States to find a band he considered good enough to play the music for a film that was to be made in England by the Rank Film Organisation, starring Sid Field. Camarata heard the band when he went to the BBC where they were broadcasting. He was highly impressed with the Ted Heath Band, and decided there and then that it was exactly what he was looking for. This was great news for Ted and looked like the salvation he had been praying for. There was only one snag though - a big one. Tutti wanted the band, but he himself was contracted to conduct the scores himself. Ted was shattered and all the old fears and inferiority complexes hit him - he was not wanted. But Camarata, a kind and sensitive man, and a brilliant musician understood how hard this had hurt Ted and they came to an agreement that Ted's name be billed in the film's credits, but that Tutti would conduct the band and Ted would be paid a small amount to stand by. The musicians were extremely well paid, in fact they called the Rank Organisation 'The Mint' and the value of working with Camarata was invaluable. The experience they all gained and the knowledge that Ted reaped was a salient point in the whole arrangement. The film 'London Town' was not a great success, but the music was terrific. Camarata and Ted became good friends and stayed friends afterwards - Ted taught him to play golf, and many lost golf balls later, Tutti became a keen golfer. The band, the love of Ted's life survived, thanks to Tutti Camarata.

Tutti remained a kind and thoughtful friend throughout the years, especially during Ted's long illness. After Ted died, he was still loving and caring for Moira and her family

Ted and Tutti Camarata

Chapter 40

The royalties of 'Lovely Weekend' were still coming in and the huge success of 'I'm Gonna Love that Guy' in the U.S.A. were the financial support Ted needed to keep going. It was never easy though. At one point, times were so hard that Ted could not see a way out. It was the year of 1949. A beautiful hot, sunny summer. The year that Ted and Moira's son, Nicholas was born in the March, and the year that Ted had bought 'Oakfield' a huge house at the top of Copse Hill, Wimbledon. They had been looking for a bigger house than Oak Cottage from sheer necessity.

Raymond, Ted's eldest son had tuberculosis contracted during his national service in the army and was due out of the sanatorium after twenty two months, to recuperate at home. In those days, TB was a long terrible illness, which entailed sanatorium treatment for anything up to two years. This obviously meant Ray having his own bedroom. No longer could the three boys, Ray, Bobby and Martin share. Ted's mother was also living with them and Moira was pregnant with Nicholas. A larger house than Oak Cottage was essential. Ted came home one day and told Moira he had bought a house. He said, "the view is out of this world, you can see for miles around. It does need quite a lot of doing to it. And it is big". Big! It was enormous. Seventeen rooms, ten bedrooms, two bathrooms, and a large basement with several rooms. Four floors, counting the basement. But Ted was right. The view was fantastic. On a clear day you could see Epsom Grandstand. And looking over the surrounding areas was like being on the top of a mountain. At night, one could see all the yellow street lights leading to Croydon, and from the day nursery, the children could watch the little trains (they were not little but appeared to be), running below like toys. The view was certainly magnificent.

But the house was in a bad state. The kitchen was filthy, thick grease on every surface. It was painted maroon red and needed hard scrubbing, stripping and painting to make it liveable. Moira was aghast. "I'll never be able to make a home from this big barn of a place" she said. They had no curtains, no carpets, except one large rug from Oak Cottage, and no money. It did, however, become, after much loving care, the family home and the Heaths pride and joy. Ted's vision was pretty well right, though Moira, deep in her heart thought he could have let her see it first before buying it. One of Ted's foibles.

With the house came a sow with 14 piglets, which was an ideal interest and hobby for Ray. That hobby became eventually a small pig farm, right in the middle of Wimbledon. Ted had modern sties built, with infra red heating, and bought a prize sow and a prize boar and soon there were a hundred pigs, which Ray used to sell, in Guildford market.

'Oakfield' had land consisting of a garden, and a field, in all, two and a half acres. In the field was a sty, and it was surrounded by an electric fence. He employed two young lads, called 'Tish' and 'Tosh' to help Ray.

One fine day, a Sunday, Ted and Moira were expecting guests for tea, Moira dressed up in a silk dress and white shoes, when there was an unbelievable hullabaloo from the sties. The family rushed down the garden to see what was the matter, and found a sow in great distress, her eyes wild and red, trying to batter her way into a sty, where her babies had been put. She was in agony with her milk, as the piglets had been taken from her too soon. The piglets were squealing to get to her, and all the other pigs had taken up the chorus.

Moira and Martin took up a rake and hoe, and gently tried to coerce the sow away from the gate of the sty, so that Val could open it and let the sow get to her young. This, they managed to do, and the poor sow and her babies were quietened and content.

Meanwhile, a large crowd had gathered, apparently the noise had been heard as far away as Raynes Park and to their horror, they found that the black sow and her babies, ten in all, had broken down the electric fence, crossed the road, and were wandering in the recreation ground below, digging up the dahlias! Ray was away for the weekend, and Tish and Tosh were off duty. There was nothing else to do, except for Moira, Martin, Val and Bijou, their black miniature poodle (poodles are game dogs when they are allowed to be natural, instead of lap dogs), to chase down to the recreation ground and herd the sow and piglets back, out of the gardens, across the road and back into the field. Ted, meanwhile, was mending the fence. It must have been a sight to see, almost like a scene from Monty Python and the crowd who had gathered to watch this Sunday afternoon entertainment by the Heaths were highly amused.

Chapter 41

The pig saga was a story in itself. The first sow to produce piglets decided to have them at 2 o'clock in the morning. The whole Heath family went down to the sty, armed with hot water bottles, rubber gloves and Dettol to help her. Of course, she did not need help. The little piglets popped out in their silken cauls, one after the other, seventeen in all. The sad part of it was that while she was feeding them, she rolled on to one, and damaged his leg. The little chap became a doted on pet, and Moira and Val were feeding him with one of the baby Nicholas' bottles of Cow and Gate baby food. He thrived and grew but a three legged pig is under too much of a disadvantage and after a few weeks, they reluctantly had to let the veterinary surgeon put him down.

The Family at Oakfield

Chapter 42

Meanwhile, to go back to the move from Oak Cottage to Oakfield. They were unhappy to leave the cottage, which had been home for fifteen years, especially Martin, who was dreadfully upset, but set about the Herculean task of making Oakfield into a habitable family home. Moira went to Harrods auction rooms to buy second-hand curtains and bits of furniture and picked up some real bargains. The professional dealers got to know her, and were very helpful and friendly.

Two months after the move, Nicholas was born in a nursing home on Parkside, Wimbledon. A beautiful blonde baby boy. That lovely sunny summer of 1949 was perfect for a baby to grow brown and healthy, and to enjoy the garden but business was disastrous. People were enjoying the long warm summer evenings out of doors, and the regular fans following the Band was still in infant form. Ted became terribly depressed and at one point said to Moira, when she was in the garden with the baby "come inside, and be miserable with me".

This did not last too long. Ted's fighting spirit and belief in his band was not going to be defeated. A Scottish Italian restaurateur Mr. Domenico, with two delightful daughters, Lydia and Norma, was keen for Lydia, who had a beautiful pure singing voice, to have a chance as a professional band singer. He asked Ted to listen to her, and as Ted was looking for a girl singer, she became Ted's first regular female vocalist. Ted decided her stage name should be Lydia McDonald. She was a delightful girl but with her gentle way and upbringing, not suited to the hard life of band touring and stage appearances. She was painfully shy, and eventually gave up the whole experience. The Domenico family remained good friends however - Mrs. Domenico was Nicholas' godmother and later on, Peter Chilvers, who played guitar with the band, married Norma.

To return to the dire financial situation in 1949, Mr. Domenico offered to lend Ted two thousand pounds to help him out. This was a godsend, and helped to keep the band together over those summer months. Ted managed to pay it back in the autumn, but was very grateful to Mr. Domenico for his kindness. The local tradespeople too, were most kind and helpful. Moira asked them if they would allow them credit until things improved and the butcher, greengrocer and dairy all knew and respected the Heaths and kindly agreed.

When stereo was first introduced, Ted had one specially made. The player was like a large old fashioned, gramophone, placed at one end of their large drawing room, and the loud speaker was at the other end. The room was 36 feet long. The loudspeaker was custom made like a gentleman's wardrobe, four inches thick of solid oak, so there was no vibration. Ted adored it, and would stand close to it with the music at full blast. It was the equivalent of being in front of the band. He would say to Moira 'Listen to this', and she would have to go into the hall, and sit half way up their large staircase, to listen to his latest recording. The density of sound being too much for her ears. No wonder, Ted lost some of his hearing later on in life. He lost an octave of sound, but it didn't' prevent him from hearing every note and nuance. It only affected his ability to hear the human voice, especially Moira's soft voice. He was really quite wicked though, because when he was bored with someone, he used his deafness as an excuse to move politely away.

Moira and Val sometimes, to trick him, would stand behind him and say something about him. He would immediately turn round and say 'I heard that' and they would all laugh. He had a hearing aid fixed into his spectacles, but most of the time, he carried them in his briefcase, too proud to use them.

Occasionally the volume on the hearing aid would be turned up to its strongest pitch and he would walk around with the thing screeching away, everybody around, wondering what on earth the noise was.

Garden at Oakfield – Nick, Tim, Moira and Ted

Chapter 43

In the early fifties, the band became a huge success. The musicians that Ted gathered round him, were the best. Highly talented, and enthusiastic and the dance halls where they played were packed. The fans would stand in front of the bandstand, listening and watching their idols. It was a sight to see. This huge mass of people, just standing and swaying to the exciting music. The keen dancers in the background, dancing to their heart's content.

The band worked seven nights a week, playing dances and concerts. Paul Carpenter was the brilliant compere and singer (in the Sinatra style) and it is absolutely true that the girl fans swooned at his feet!

From then on, Ted's courage and belief in himself did not desert him. He started the Sunday night concerts at the Palladium in London, thanks to Jack Parnell (a staunch and loyal member of the band, from the early years, to the present day, twenty nine years after Ted died) who spoke to his uncle, Val Parnell, who owned the Palladium and Moss Empires, asking that Ted could hire the Palladium. There were no regular Sunday concerts up to then, and Ted's concerts became a fantastic success, with the fans, turning up in their hundreds to hear the band, every third Sunday. The same seats were booked for each show, and the same loyal people were there every show.

Ted had meanwhile come to a very important decision. He needed to broaden the band's appeal to audiences all over the country. Although the band on its own, held the same drawing power it always had, the entertainment value needed to be extended and the answer was to have vocalists. Ted could not have been luckier than to find Dickie Valentine, a delightful and charming young man, with a lovely voice and personality, who up until then was virtually unknown as Richard Bryce. Ted decided that Dickie Valentine would be a good name for his boy singer to join Paul Carpenter, a fine compere and singer already with the band and Jack Parnell, who took on occasional vocals as well as being the band's drummer. Dickie, was immensely popular with the girl fans from the start, a fabulous performer with a myriad of fans who followed the band wherever it went to hero worship him. He added an enormous attraction to the shows and was just what Ted had wanted, a young legend was born. He remained one of Ted and Moira's closest friends, until his tragic death in a car accident, fifteen months after Ted's death.

The next stroke of luck for Ted was the approach of Lita Roza, who wanted to sing with the band. Ted was so impressed with her singing and stage presence at

**Ted, Nick and Jack Parnell -
London Palladium**

**Ted with his two youngest
sons, Nicholas and Timothy**

Lita Roza

Dickie Valentine and Dennis Lotis

The great man

her audition, that he asked her to appear, there and then at the next Sunday concert. She proved to be the perfect addition to Dickie, also singing duets with Jack Parnell. She was glamour personified and sexy, with a cheeky sense of humour and was a big success throughout the years she was with the band

To complete the vocal line-up, a young man from South Africa had decided to seek his fortune in England and Dennis Lotis was just right. A great singer, wonderful personality, a 'dreamboat' and still appearing with the band to the present day - loyal and loving.

So the unforgettable singers with the Ted Heath Band were to become part of the best British band there had ever been.

Jack Parnell, the original drummer with the band was also a very fine personality and singer and at times, joined the vocal force, singing solo and duets with Lita Roza. One of the trumpet players too, Dave Wilkins would sing in his own inimitable style, and Duncan Campbell brought joy and laughter to both the musicians and the audiences. This enormous bevy of talent and glamour increased the reputation and popularity of the band.
Later, when Dickie had left the band to go 'solo' Bobby Britton joined the band. A fine singer and good looking too. He was always ready to enter into any ideas for the concerts that were put up. One successful and funny scene was Bobby singing 'You've got to have 'Hair' instead of 'Heart', wearing an atrocious wig and framed in a gold picture frame. It was quite hilarious and caused a lot of laughter.

Jackie Armstrong and Duncan Campbell were the funny men – sometimes singing excruciating parodies of opera, or doing unmentionable things when inspecting the chairs they were going to sit on, much to the amusement of the audience.
Johnny Hawksworth was his own unusual and special self, virtually being a solo act with comedy and brilliant bass playing. Kenny Baker led his own group which gave a different element to the concert, and Jack Parnell, wonderful drummer and charismatic band leader, led another group to add a further dimension. Additionally, there were great artists to give an added thrill. Of course, too, Paul Carpenter gave his own particular gloss and charm with his announcing and singing.

At one particular show, the curtain was down, the house lights lowered and Jack Bentley, one of the trombone players, pulled a chair on to the stage, in front of the curtain, sat down with his 'cello' and droned away, some forgettable unknown tune, much to the amusement of the audience. Then the curtain was raised and some of the musicians ambled on stage talking amongst themselves and ignoring the audience. Then Jack Parnell sat down at the piano and started to play a little jazz. Bobby Pratt went to the drums and other musicians joined in, busking. It was a wonderful start and different to the normal concert. After a short spell, the stage lights went up and Ted walked on – The concert proper began with Ted's signature tune 'Listen to my Music.

On the hundredth, the first half closed with 'Farewell Blues'. The latest addition to join the band played a solo and walked off stage. This went on, with each musician according to his length of stay with the band, playing a solo and walking off. Eventually there were only two left, Les Gilbert the saxophone player, and Jimmy Coombes, bass trombone, and Ted. Les played his piece, which left Jimmy Coombes as the last to play, as the longest serving member of the band. At that time bass trombonists very seldom got to play solos, so it was a great thrill for Jimmy. He played then walked off, leaving Ted standing alone, with just the spotlight on him. It was very moving and an emotive finish to the first half of the concert. It brought a lump to the throats of many of the fans there.

Another great idea of Ted's was to have sixteen small drums made, one for each musician. Ronnie Verrall, the brilliant drummer with the band at that time, played his drums and the different sections of the band, answered him on their small drums. It built up to a most exciting drum solo with Ronnie, and a never to be forgotten finale to the show. The number was 'Rhapsody for Drums'. A great climax.

Incidentally, Ronnie asked Moira if he could 'borrow' the drums when he later joined the Syd Lawrence Orchestra, and I believe they still perform it on some of their concerts.

Another of Ted's inspired ideas was to have ultra violet lamps set up on the stage. The musicians wore white gloves, which were made luminous with the 'U.V's and did various hand movements to the music. Their white shirts also showed up luminous and their faces black. The effect was electric. At the thrilling end of the number 'Jungle Drums', Ronnie Verrall, whose drum sticks were also luminous, threw several, one after the other up in the air, and some to the audience. A truly wonderful piece of stage magic, thought up by Ted. It must be said, that to put on these concerts, there were only two men to handle the equipment and set up stage and the band manager and the electricians of the venue where they were playing. Unlike today, where the 'bands'! Of two, three and four musicians have an army of people to set them up. Admittedly, there were occasionally problems, such as a last minute panic with the ultra violet lamps, but the show went on.

An early picture of the Band

An amusing episode happened at the Chiswick Empire. Dickie Valentine, wonderfully handsome and attractive in a kilt, was singing 'Down in the Glen'. The idea was to have a Scottish mist rising gently up around him. The only snag was that the machine that made the mist, failed to work properly. By the end of the song, Dickie had almost disappeared in the mist, and the machine could not blow it away. The next number was a South American number 'Peanut Vendor' which rather lost its atmosphere of sunshine, heat and tropical glamour, as it was still shrouded in Scottish mist! It caused a great deal of amusement and the musicians found it difficult not to laugh, but Ted was not a happy man. Being a perfectionist, he was, to say the least, not pleased that a mere machine could spoil a perfect production.

The three vocalists proved the icing on the cake for the Ted Heath Band, and took it into the success years of the 1950s. The Sunday concerts were marvellous. Many guest stars appeared with the band, notably among them, the Johnny Dankworth Seven (one of their first breaks) Ray Ellington and his Quartet, Petula Clark in schoolgirl clothes and socks! And the exciting and thrilling Ella Fitzgerald. Ella had been appearing at the Palladium during the week in variety and was unhappy and depressed at the reception she was receiving from the regular variety audiences. She was singing songs like 'Woody Woodpecker Song' and not showing her fantastic talent. Ted called round back stage to ask her to appear on his swing session. At first, she and her husband were adamant that she would not do it. But after an hour or so, Ted persuaded them that she would have an audience like she had never had before. The subsequent concert she appeared in was a night to remember always. The audience took her to their hearts and raved over her. The dress circle (balcony) actually had to be checked for safety the following week, because the swaying and stamping of feet might have weakened it. This delightful woman was so happy and pleased, she jumped up and down and flung her arms around Ted's neck and kissed him.

The Sunday Swing sessions reached over a hundred performances and only stopped to give way to television's Sunday Night at the Palladium.

On the 100th Palladium concert, the musicians presented Ted with a beautiful silver salver, inscribed with a drawing of his face, and the words:

A tribute to a Gentleman
A token of thanks in silver

To

Ted Heath
A great leader

From all the boys in the Band

1945-1954

On the occasion of his
100th Concert
At the
London Palladium

Moira was presented with a huge bouquet, a lovely jewel case with a gold trombone charm in it and a card saying 'with love from the Orchestra Wives'.

Moira and Ted with the Silver Salver presentation from the Band

Chapter 44

Once again, Ted had proved his belief in the band, and chanced his arm. The concerts were an instant success and were always full to capacity right up to the last one, one hundred and eight concerts later.

These concerts, every third week, were to create a following for the band that was phenomenal. Fans booked the same seats for every show, (a few of the girl fans would even copy Moira's hat styles) and the crowds would gather outside the stage door to hero worship. This was long before the Beatles appeared on the scene. At some of the theatres around the country, the crowds were so great, that mounted police were on duty to keep control. None of this was stage managed or publicity 'hyped'. It was a completely natural expression of the appreciation of the fans for the musicians and singers. Certainly, some very enthusiastic young ones would scream and try to touch or grab something belonging to the object of their delight. Ted regularly lost cuff links taken from his sleeves and handkerchiefs from his breast pocket. So much so, that Moira eventually bought him cheap cuff links and sewed his very expensive hand rolled linen handkerchiefs into the pockets. His zip fastener on his trousers was occasionally a source of attraction to the girls, and consequently an embarrassment to him.

At one concert at the Albert Hall in London, the house was full and Moira was happy for some fans to join her in her box. The girls were wild about Dickie Valentine, tearing their handkerchiefs to shreds, tears streaming down their cheeks, and screaming "Dickie, Dickie".

At Hammersmith Palais, where the band did a regular Monday night dance, the crowds were immense, and long queues formed outside waiting to get in. Moira always sat upstairs in the balcony, and she was usually joined by Pauline Carpenter Paul's delightful wife, and Kay Kendall, a beautiful young film star, who at that time was Jack Parnell's girlfriend. She later died, tragically young. The girls were always dressed up to the nines - big hats and beautiful clothes. This was a long time, before jeans became the universal uniform.

At these dances many, young American servicemen, especially sailors, would dance the jitter-bug, hitherto unknown in Britain, some dancing together but mostly picking up the pretty girl fans, and creating an exciting new dimension to the evenings.

The Band performing at the Hammersmith Palais

Chapter 45

Once Ted was asked to play for a dance at Windsor Castle. He was delighted to accept, but when it came to discussing the fee, he was told 'But we don't pay for it, old man. You do it for the honour'. The honour, yes, was fine for Ted, but it was the musician's bread and butter. If they had done all the 'honour' jobs for nothing, they would not be able to survive. Ted did offer to do several charitable concerts, mainly for the Variety Club of Great Britain, and the Musicians Benevolent Society, for which he naturally received no fee, but paid the musicians their normal fee from his own pocket. But much as he admired the monarchy, he did not consider them a charity.

It is to be wondered, if that was the reason why he was never given an honour, although other bandleaders, such as Victor Silvester received the OBE.

When Ted was ill, Moira wrote to Harold Wilson, the then Prime Minister, saying how thrilled Ted would be to receive even an MBE in recognition of his work for British dance music, over the years. He had flown the British flag all over the world and was so proud of being British, and of his British musicians. He was sent a letter signed by a secretary, to say they regretted it could not be fitted in.

Well! Perhaps he had trodden on someone's toes.

Chapter 46

During Ted's career as a bandleader, he was honoured to have been chosen twice for the Royal Command Performances. The first time was in front of King George VI and Queen Elizabeth, and the second for the present Queen and the Duke of Edinburgh, both at the London Palladium.

Among the many great international artistes chosen was Danny Kaye, a great favourite of the Royal family but like many of these stars being on personal relations with them, he made the mistake of showing familiarity towards the Royal box during his act. This was a special privilege allowed to very few. The Crazy Gang spring to mind, with their loveable but cheeky act - Danny Kaye was not amongst the favoured few - he left the stage to almost total silence, no applause and went back stage in tears. He said to Ted "what did I do wrong?" He had broken the unwritten code. The audiences at the Command Performances were notoriously difficult. To put it in stage terms, they 'sat on their hands' (unlike the normal audiences who were generous with their applause) and poor Danny Kaye suffered. He had played to the Royal box, and even introduced his wife in the stalls. Simply, it was not done.

The Palladium concerts opened up a whole new era of band entertainment on Sunday evenings and eventually there were many bands doing the same thing, and of course, still are to the present day. The 'Ted Heath Swing Sessions' were always sold out. Ted came up with some brilliant new ideas for the shows, and there were new arrangements every performance. The musicians also had excellent ideas to create an entertaining show.

Chapter 47

In 1951 Timothy was born in the same Parkside Wimbledon Nursing Home as Nicholas. Moira had been extraordinarily well throughout the pregnancy. This baby was so much wanted as Moira and Ted felt that Nicholas might become very spoilt, being adored by them and especially by Val, almost like an only child.

Tim was, like his brothers and sister, an incredibly beautiful baby. They decided he would be the last and laughingly suggested 'Ultimo' as a suitable name. As it was, they named him 'Timothy Edward Dee' so he was the small Ted Heath. Being older parents, they treasured their two little sons and Ted was able to spend more time (and money!) with them, than he had been able to with Martin and Val. They also considered themselves very fortunate to have such a clever recipe for producing lovely children. God was good.

Chapter 48

The band became enormously popular, not only in Great Britain but also overseas. Wherever they went, Ted flew the flag. The uniforms, the musicians wore were royal blue, with badges on their pockets in gold thread and red embroidery. The bandstands were red, white and blue and he stressed everywhere on their tours, that the band was totally British and proud of it.

They were invited to tour Australia, a massive undertaking. At every appearance they were enthusiastically received but the financial overheads were huge and the tour was not really a viable proposition. It was though a terrific personal success for Ted and the musicians and a 'never to be forgotten' experience.

The Australian Tour

A tour of Australia and New Zealand was arranged, mainly due to the enthusiasm of Jack Neary, the Australian promoter, who had heard Ted Heath and his Music at the London Palladium.

They duly left England in March 1955, on what was another big experience for the band. Ted's fears that Jack Neary's optimism about the success of a British band would be a sell out, were well founded. They played to wonderfully enthusiastic audiences, but there were too many empty seats. This did not daunt Jack Neary and his colleagues, and he said that a return visit would prove his point and it was all worth it. The cost of the whole project was enormous, but the band were fully paid and had their 'round the world' air ticket, fully ensured. The promoters deserved well earned praise and a long standing admiration of their honest ways of doing business, and their faith in presenting what they believed was the best in big band music.

Lita Roza and Dickie Valentine had left the band a few months earlier, to follow their own careers as solo artistes, so the difficult task of replacing them ensued. A young and beautiful girl called Kathy Lloyd saw Ted at his London office. She had entered a contest for girl singers to find a replacement for Lita Roza. She won the Zinger Girl Contest, and Ted was delighted to have found another lovely vocalist. The replacement for Dickie Valentine was not easy. His popularity and success was enormous, but Ted was lucky in finding a young man called Michael Day, re-christened by Ted, as Bobbie Britton. He had an outstanding voice, was very good looking and was keen and eager to do well. His rather shy personality was in contrast to Dickie's, but he made a name for himself and was very popular. The vocalist line up for the Australian tour was Dennis Lotis, Kathy Lloyd and Bobbie Britton, all exceedingly attractive and talented.

The journey to Australia was rather too eventful. They were delayed at Heathrow for several hours, arriving very late at Karachi. They were delayed many hours there. Before going on to Singapore where there was to be an eight hour stay at the Raffles Hotel. Kicking their heels, Ted was getting more and more worried that they might not arrive in Sydney in time for their first concert. He needed the band to rehearse and thought the ballroom would be suitable, but the ambience of the old fashioned Raffles Hotel was hardly the place for a large, loud, swing band. This created a situation, whereby the rehearsal had to be called off, which led to some adverse comments in the Australian press, saying that the

Ted, Paul Carpenter and Bobbie Britton

Band was thrown out of the hotel, because of the noise! Quite untrue, they cancelled the rehearsal quite voluntarily.

They finally took off for Sydney, several hours late. An amusing incident happened when a very attractive stewardess appeared, who had to make the announcements. The musicians, with their great sense of humour, and appreciation of female beauty, applauded her, every time she spoke. The rest of the passengers took it up, those travelling by air for the first time, thinking it was the usual custom. Ted often wondered if it set up a trend on that particular airline. During that flight, they experienced a rather frightening plunge downwards of a hundred and fifty feet, due to a fall in air pressure, but no one was hurt, and no damage was done. They thankfully arrived in Sydney, two hours before the concert was due to begin.

The tour was a huge success in audience appreciation, and no doubt, if they had been able to make a return visit, it would have been a financial success.

They visited Sydney, Melbourne, Adelaide, Brisbane, Newcastle and on to New Zealand. Ted had many happy memories of the hospitality and warmth of the people he met.

Ted had asked Kenny Graham to compose an Australian Suite for the tour. This Kenny did, and wrote some wonderful tunes. The best known was 'Kings Cross Climax'. 'Lovers on Bondi Beach' and 'When a Bodgie meets a Widgie' were also popular. 'Lovers on Bondi Beach' was an exceptionally lovely piece of music and Ted asked Moira to put words to it. A difficult task, but she achieved it.

Johnny Mathis liked the song very much, it hardly became a hit. Ted re-named it 'Beaulieu Abbey', in honour of the band's appearance at the outdoor concert at Lord Montague's home 'Beaulieu' and it remained one of his most favourite tunes for the rest of his life.

After the tour, the band had a break, and most of them took the opportunity to use their round the world air tickets, to visit various places.

Ted stayed in Honolulu for a few days, then went on to Hollywood. There, he met Ray Anthony, Billy May and Les Brown, who showed him delightful hospitality, before joining Moira and the children in Miami. Altogether a never to be forgotten experience for him, and one of the highlights of his life.

Whilst the band was in Australia, Ted had wanted Moira to take Val, Nick and Tim, who all three had suffered whooping cough, to recuperate in the sun. Ted, as usual, was kind and caring and wanted the best for his family. Moira and the children left for America in the prestigious ocean liner, the Queen Mary. During the voyage, Moira was invited to the purser's cocktail party. Val was upset not to be asked, and Moira mentioned it to the purser. He was surprised to learn that Val was seventeen. He had thought she was only seven, as the other children Nick and Tim were five and three respectively. He immediately put things right and Val had a good time for the rest of the voyage with the young officers. When they arrived in New York, the drummer of the ship's band, asked to take her to Birdland that evening. It was a big thrill for her and she was introduced to Dizzy Gillespie.

After a few days in New York, going up the Empire State Building and generally sightseeing, they took the Orange Blossom Express down to Miami. Thinking the journey would be like the movies, and that Tommy Dorsey's Band would be on board. It was anything but that. The compartment was very hot during the day, and freezing cold at night. The food and service was dire. The carriage was literally 'rolling stock' and the children were very sick. They discovered what 'the other side of the tracks' meant. Unlike Britain, the train travelled through the poorest parts of the country with shanty towns on either side and it proved to be twenty six hours of misery, not the glamorous journey they had expected.

They arrived in Miami and checked into the Roney Plaza Hotel on Miami Beach. It was like an enormous wedding cake, where they stayed for two weeks.

Moira saw that both Tommy Dorsey and his brother Jimmy Dorsey were the bands playing at the Fontainbleu Hotel. This was a perfect opportunity to meet Tommy Dorsey, Ted's hero. She arranged for a babysitter to look after Nick and Tim and booked a table for herself and Val. This was a wonderful experience to hear the two famous bands, and when Tommy, who had been told she was in the audience, came over to her table and spoke to her, she was over the moon. He was a delightful man, charming and courteous. He said the band was doing a session the next day, and would she like to be there. Of course, there was no hesitation until he said the session was in New York. He was very amused when she told him of their twenty six hour journey on the Orange Blossom Express. He said "I have my private plane, and I will fly you and the kids there and back", but she thought discretion was the better part of valour, and that Ted would be upset if she had accepted. As it was, when he telephoned her from Australia, he was quite envious that she had met the great Tommy Dorsey before he had. Of course, he met him in New York later.

Moira and the children went on to Jamaica for the sunshine the children needed so much. Ted telephoned nearly every day, but the lines were very bad, and it was frustrating for them both. All they really heard was 'hello, hello' and 'goodbye'.

They arranged to meet at the Roney Plaza in Miami when Ted returned from Australia. Moira felt that Jamaica was a little laid back for Ted, who did not enjoy lying on a beach, doing nothing.

Ted went to Miami via Honolulu and Hollywood. When he rejoined the family, they stayed in Miami for a few days and then flew to New York. No more long train journeys for them. In New York, they visited many of the jazz clubs and enjoyed meeting and hearing Eddie Condon at his club

Ted met Tommy Dorsey there and many other famous musicians and then took a plane home to England. Moira and the children travelled back on the Queen Elizabeth, the sister ship to the Queen Mary. During that voyage, George Shearing, the famous blind pianist, was on board. He was delighted to meet Ted's family, and remained friends over the years.

Ted, relaxing in the sun

Chapter 49

The first tour of the Ted Heath Band to the States was being discussed. There was a big obstacle to be overcome. The American Federation of Musicians had refused to allow British bands to work there. In retaliation, the Musicians Union of Great Britain had put up the ban on American bands. Ted had met Stan Kenton, the most progressive American bandleader of all time, and the idea was mooted, that there should be an exchange of the Kenton Band and the Heath Band. They were limited to playing only concerts, but it opened the doors, so that later, many great American bands appeared in Britain and British bands, including the Beatles were allowed to appear in the States. An important step in musical history.

The first American tour was set to open in San Antonio in Texas.

Ted decided, typically, that the band should travel to America in style. Nothing but the best in British ships would be their means of arrival. The renowned and prestigious Queen Mary was to take them to New York. The cost of this form of luxury travel was enormous, but Ted felt that it was important to impress the Americans, that this was a band of great prestige, flying the British flag. He was helped by E.R. Lewis (later Sir Edward Lewis) Chairman of Decca Records, and their American counterpart London Records.

Much to Ted's delight, Henry Cotton, the champion British golfer, was on board, and he and Ted became friends.

On arrival in New York, the band rehearsed for three days and the musicians had the opportunity to visit the night spots and hear the great bands and the talents of their fellow American musicians and meet some of the top bandleaders.

Among them, Benny Goodman. During the evening, Benny announced that a great British bandleader, Ted Heath was dining there. Unfortunately, Ted had to rush off to be interviewed for a broadcast, and had left Moira and his party still there. When Benny realised that there was no Ted Heath there he laughed and said, "Where is he?" One of the band said he had gone to "the little boy's room" which caused much amusement. Benny's playing was very relaxed. He sat on a stool in front of his band and as always, played his clarinet beautifully.

After the evening session at the Waldorf Astoria, Benny invited Ted (who had rejoined his party) and Moira up to his penthouse apartment. He was charming and very interested in Ted's forthcoming tour.

On board the Queen Mary for the first American Tour: Johnny Keating, Henry MacKenzie, Wally Smith, Ric Kennedy Don Lusher

The band flew down to Texas and arrived in San Antonio for the rehearsal for the first concert of the tour. Carlos Gastel, who promoted the show, told Ted that they would be playing three numbers. Ted was aghast. No way had they travelled thousands of miles to play a paltry seven minutes. They could not hope to make any impression whatsoever, and he was adamant that he would not appear at all, if that was Carlos Gastel's decision.

After a complete impasse, with everybody hanging around in utter misery, it was at last decided that the Ted Heath Band would play the whole of the first half of the show with June Christy and the Four Freshmen. They would then play the opening number of the second half to introduce Nat King Cole and his Trio, whom they were very happy to accompany. June Christy, the Four Freshmen and Nat Cole completely understood Ted's feelings and were very co-operative to work with the band. The show was a great success and the papers next day were full of praise.

The tour was tougher than any the Band had previously experienced. The distances travelled by bus (coach) were enormous and involved travelling all night. They packed up after the concerts, got on the bus and travelled through the night. The camaraderie of the Four Freshmen and June and the musicians was fantastic. Constant jokes and laughter, and a complete rapport. Moira acted as unofficial dresser to June, who was hopelessly untidy. She would pick June's clothes up off the dressing room floor and hang them up and see June on to the stage, looking stunningly beautiful with everything in place. She and Moira remained friends until her sad death. Bob Flanagan of the Freshmen also remained friends, and he and Moira met up again when he visited London in 1995, just before his retirement.

The tour included New Orleans, a dream come true for the British musicians, who had looked forward so much to hearing the various jazz groups there. It was a question of staying up all night, visiting the clubs and having coffee next morning on the banks of the Mississippi, near the riverboats. Incidentally, the Mississippi is quite brown and muddy! Not a beautiful green and blue water vision.

During the tour of the Deep South, the problem of racism reared its ugly head. Nat Cole and his Trio could not travel or stay in the same hotels as the white artistes. They stayed in hotels outside the towns and travelled separately.

The show consisted of two concerts a night. The first concert was for white audiences and the second, after midnight, for coloured audiences, which had to be acceptable to Ted, as there was no choice. But it upset him and his musicians very much to have to agree to have a gauze curtain between Nat King Cole and his Trio and the white musicians on stage. When they got to Birmingham, Alabama the first half of the show went down so well and the white audience was so enthusiastic. Ted suggested to the stage manager that the gauze curtain should be lifted. Almost immediately five men with sawn-off shot guns had jumped up on the stage, punched Nat Cole, broke the microphone and attacked the bass player and guitarist. The atmosphere was terrifying and the whole mood of the concert was spoiled. Most of the audience were applauding Nat and trying to make up for the appalling behaviour of the few fanatics. Nat returned to the stage, and although visibly shaken, he acted with the innate dignity that was his, and said he had been born in Alabama and he knew they wanted to hear him sing and play. He did the second show, and received a rapturous reception from the coloured audience.

For the rest of the tour in the South, there were armed guards back stage and the Ted Heath Band had their name removed from the bus they travelled on in case there might be a retaliatory attack on Ted - but there was no further trouble. June and the Freshmen were terribly upset and kept on telling the British guys, that they were as disgusted as everybody and that this was not the general attitude of the American people. There was, however, great relief when they reached towns above the Mason Dixon line, and Nat and the musicians could get together again after the show.

The culmination of the tour was, of course, the concert at the Carnegie Hall in New York. The band would be the first British band to play there and it was to be the whole show for the Ted Heath Band. The place was packed and there were many of the famous American band leaders and musicians there to hear this fabulous British band, including Tommy Dorsey, Benny Goodman, Duke Ellington, Count Basie et al. One fan said to Ted, "You must have mostly Americans in your band". Ted replied proudly "I have no Americans in my band but we do have seven Scotsmen".

The concert was an outstanding success. The musicians, as they always did, brought out that magical extra, playing beautifully and at the end, the applause was deafening. Ted turned to the musicians and applauded them. Tears of emotion were very near. In spite of their weariness after the gruelling travelling, it made it all worthwhile and one of the highest peaks in the history of the band.

It cannot just be written about as a 'one off' though. The band, throughout the whole of its long career, and now to the present day, have that special magic and charisma that places them among the stars.

They returned home to Southampton on the Queen Elizabeth. For the first twenty four hours of the voyage, nothing was seen of any of them. They were so exhausted and although Ted and Moira were invited to sit at the Captain's table (an honour) they begged off, and sat at a table nearby. Moira said that all she ate the whole journey home was caviar and asparagus. Not exactly a hardship, but a change from the Howard Johnson sandwiches swimming in gravy, which had been staple diet on the road!

The itinerary of the tour was:

San Antonio,	*Texas*
Fort Worth,	*Texas*
Houston,	*Texas*
New Orleans,	*Louisiana*
Mobile,	*Alabama*
Birmingham,	*Alabama*
Raleigh,	*Virginia*
Columbus,	*South Carolina*
Elkhart,	*Indiana*
Erie,	*New York*
Rochester,	*New York*
Pittsburgh,	*Pennsylvania*
Charlestown,	*Virginia*
Washington DC	
Carnegie Hall,	*New York*

Ted and Nat King Cole

Chapter 50

On arrival home, the musical press in England gave them all the tributes they deserved. They had proved that British musicians were as good as any in the world, and they had flown the flag. The years of success had started, wherever the band played, to name a few, Hammersmith Palais, Imperial Ballroom Blackpool, Torquay, Manchester, Glasgow, people crowded round the bandstand, and stood and listened to every single note, in rapt attention. The dancers, and let it not be said that 'you could not dance to Ted Heath', were happy to have plenty of floor space at the back to dance.

To prove a point, the band was booked to play a three month stint at the Savoy Hotel in London. Ted had a lot of new arrangements written, mainly following the old Ambrose adage, that you must hear the dancers feet on the floor while the band is playing. Everybody said "my God! Ted Heath at the Savoy, he'll blow the roof off". How wrong they were. The music was exquisite. Only really first class musicians can play very quietly with perfect tone and rhythm. The only snag was that they hated playing waltzes. In fact, Jack Parnell threatened to chuck the job in, rather than play a waltz. Ted talked him around, saying that the money was good, there was no travelling, there was time for golf and it was only for 3 months. When the Savoy management asked Ted to extend their stay to a year, he said if he accepted there would be no band.

Meanwhile, the band was getting broadcasts and some television shows. Ted had to fight all the way to get the broadcasts. Tawny Nielson, who was in charge of radio at the BBC then, asked Ted to meet her in her office, to discuss the situation. When he arrived, she said to her secretary "You can go for lunch now" but Ted said, "no, I want her to hear all I have to say". He said to Tawny, "I am not going to wine you, dine you or buy you expensive presents but you are going to have to give me broadcasts because of public demand", and stalked out of the room. Tawny told Moira some time after that she had never admired someone more - he had the courage to stand up against the system and laid his neck on the line. Well, it certainly worked!

The band won the Silver Rose at the Montreux Festival of Television and Ted was asked to play in a film at Shepperton Film Studios. It was called 'It's a Wonderful World' starring George Cole, Kathleen Harrison, Terence Morgan and William Hayter, and a very pretty young French actress called Mylene Demongeot. Ted was asked to play himself. He became known to the rest of the cast as 'One Take Ted' because he would never repeat a performance. He also used to change the script because he said it wouldn't sound right as written because it would not be natural to him. It speaks highly of the very professional actors and actresses that they could come in at the right time, even though Ted had changed the script. The photography of the band was tremendous and of course the music was excellent. Moira wrote all the lyrics, Ted the music. Dennis Lotis sang the songs. The titles of the film read, the Ted Heath Band, music by Ted Heath, lyrics by Moira Heath, Ted Heath played by himself. Quite a 'Heath' production. It was a delightful little film and has been repeated on television several times.

Ted had previously been in a film for Gaumont British called 'Dance Band' with Ted's band, Geraldo's band, Petula Clarke, Diana Dors and Shirley Ann Field

Sadly, although Hammer Films were keen to make a film of Ted's life, the financial backing was not forthcoming. The film industry in Britain was going through a bad time, Ted and Moira had a lot of fun, deciding who should play them, if the film was ever made. Their favourite choice was for Googie Withers (Moira's very dear friend) to play Moira, but the part of Ted was more difficult. He was very much an individual and not easy to depict. Who knows? One day some angel might come along and decide the story is good enough for a film.

Ted at the Savoy Hotel

Golden Rose of Montreux Festival, Cannes, France

'This is your Life'

In 1959, the BBC chose Ted to be the subject of 'This is your Life'. Anybody who has not been involved in this wonderful programme, cannot realise the enormous amount of research, careful questioning and planning to get several busy, well known people together on the night, and the innumerable 'lies' that have to be told, to explain certain unusual happenings and secret meetings, so that the honoured person (some think victim) will not be aware that they are the chosen one.

The BBC approached Moira to ask her if it would be acceptable to Ted, and if there might be any inclusions, which would cause embarrassment or unhappiness and swore her to secrecy. This, unless one has experienced it, is a somewhat traumatic, but exciting time. There were many discussions that had to take place, which necessitated Moira going into town several times, and caused amusement to Ted, who asked her why. She explained that she was going shopping, which he accepted quite happily, except for the remark that she wasn't having much luck, as there were no shopping bags around! However, he had no suspicion of what was happening, but to ensure secrecy, it was decided to have a completely 'dummy' cast.

In Ted's case, the care and trouble taken was enormous. A whole cast of another 'This is your Life' show were gathered together, having given their permission to be used as 'dummies'. Robertson Hare, the very famous actor of the Aldwych farces, and a dear friend of the Heaths, was to be the chosen star, a kind and generous gesture on his part. A complete show was put together with 'Bunny' Hare, his lovely wife Rene and daughter Diana and several friends of Bunny's acting days were gathered together, including Winifred Shotter, the female star of the famous comedies. The story, then told to Ted, was that he would be the guest on the Robertson Hare show. This explained too, the reason for Moira's absences saying she was not accustomed to being on television and needed rehearsals with Eamonn Andrews. Ted was in happy ignorance of what was to come.
On the day of the show, Moira was allowed to tell Val, Martin, Ray and Bobby that they were to appear at the Shepherds Bush Empire, that night. The two little sons, Nick and Tim, were not told then. Val rushed out to get her hair done and needless to say, there was great excitement in the family.

Ted was working all day at a session and had been told he would not be needed for rehearsal, as he was an old hand at broadcasting. To make sure, he did not get a glimpse of the children, when he arrived at the theatre, Val drove Nick and Tim round and round Shepherds Bush, until the last minute before transmission, and then they waited in the wings for the show to begin.

Shortly before the time came for transmission, Ted turned up at the theatre. He was shown into Eamonn Andrews dressing room, and there on the dressing table was a red book with 'This is your Life Robertson Hare' on it in large letters. Ted was completely relaxed and went on to the stage with a big smile and sat down with Bunny Hare's family and friends, including Moira, ready to play his part. When Eamonn Andrews went up to him, with the red book, and said 'This is your Life Ted Heath', he was struck dumb. His ears went bright red, and he was overcome with shyness.

The show then proceeded, as so carefully planned by T. Leslie Jackson, the producer, Ken Smith and Liam Nolan, the script writers, and of course the great and genial host, Eamonn Andrews.

Robertson Hare was the first to appear and delighted in showing his fondness for Ted. Moira was next to be brought on. She was very, very nervous and was afraid of forgetting her words, but Eamonn, the perfect professional, was kindness itself, and told her not to worry, he would help her through, if necessary. Such a charming and delightful man.

Then followed Al Starita, an American bandleader Ted had worked with in his early days as a musician. Al had been flown from America to appear on the show. He had arrived in England in summer clothes, suited to his home in Palm Beach and was feeling the cold. The BBC bought him warm jumpers to wear, and a very English overcoat, which delighted him. He had not seen Ted for many years, and there were many memories to talk about. He presented Ted with a gold key to the city of Palm Beach. Moira had arranged for him to stay with them in their home in Wimbledon for a week, so there was plenty of time for catching up on the years, and he enjoyed every minute of the experience.

The next guest was Harry Mortimer, an old friend of Ted's. When they were boys, they competed in the Brass Band Championships and were great rivals as well as 'mates'. His father was Fred Mortimer, great brass band leader of Fodens Band, and Harry had taken over from his father, on retirement. Harry was one of the greatest brass band musicians of all time.

Another guest was Denis Chaundy, a business man and keen golfer, who liked to be known as 'Ted's Number One Fan'. He was thrilled with the whole occasion and never wavered in his admiration and devotion to Ted.

There then followed the friends who were part of Ted's professional life. Paul Carpenter, great character, singer and compere in Ted's band. Always natural, a joker and a delightful personality. Dickie Valentine too, the romantic who was adored by the fans. Sydney Lipton, the great band leader who had been such a good friend to Ted, and had given him back his self confidence appeared next

There followed a filmed interview with Lita Roza, the beautiful girl singer with the band. She could not be present, because of a previous engagement, but she spoke charmingly to Ted.

Another guest was the old, old friend of Ted's who had played with him in his busking days, Charles Holt, a great surprise to Ted, there were many memories to exchange.

Near to the end of the show, the great Nat King Cole was shown on the screen, speaking to Ted, with great affection and admiration. Sorry that he could not be there, but he would not miss being there on Ted's 'This is your Life' for worlds.

There was also a telephone conversation with Lydia Macdonald, Ted's first singer, from Rome. She too, would have loved to be there, but she could not leave her mother, who was not very well.

Before the finale, came the entrance of Ted's children, Ray, Bobby, Martin, Val, Nick and Tim. The two little boys were literally pushed on to the stage, into the spotlight and Ted's delight in seeing his family was joyous.

The planned finale was then on show. The whole of Fodens Brass Band came on stage, Ted was handed a baton (something he never used, it was usually a tatty old silver pencil, rather chewed up!) and the music for the piece they were going to play, for Ted to conduct. The fact that the music was upside down slightly fazed him, but laughing, he turned it up the right way and conducted this wonderful brass band, thanks to Harry Mortimer.

There were only two regrets for Moira. She had wanted Stanley Matthews, England's greatest footballer, and a very close friend of Ted's, and Jack Hylton, who had been in Ted's professional life at the beginning, to be on the show.

Regretfully, they could not be included because they themselves were due to be the next subjects of 'This is your Life' in the immediate future.

It might be of interest, that the 'Red Book' handed over at the end of the show, was really a working copy. It contained the running order, and time sheets. The real red book was delivered to Ted's Berkeley House office later, enclosing pictures taken during the transmission.

Ted, principal guest with Eamonn Andrews, on "This Is Your Life", greets with pleasant surprise, his wife Moira

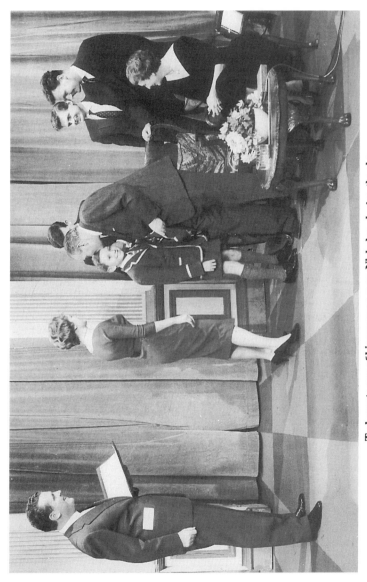

Ted greets one of his younger sons, Nicholas, during the show.
Also pictured are his daughter Val and sons Martin, Raymond and Bob.
Moira is pictured on the right.

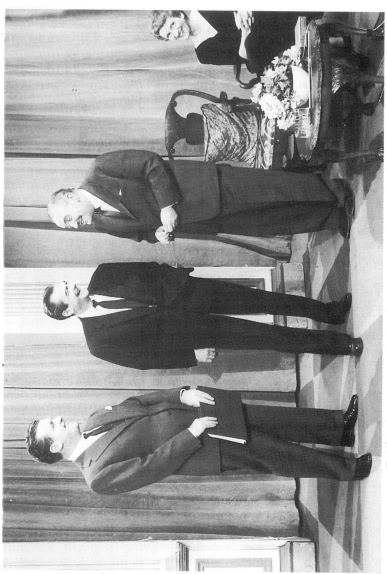

Ted listening to an amusing tale from actor/commentator Paul Carpenter

Ted receiving a "live" greeting from Rome, from Lydia MacDonald former singer with the Band

During the programme, Ted enjoys a joke with Dickie Valentine

At the end, this tribute concluded the book:

Ted Heath

Man of Music, may this book be one more tribute to an outstanding instrumentalist, star entertainer on three Continents and above all a true Gentleman

Jersey, August 1961

Moira took Nick and Tim to Jersey in the Channel Islands for a last holiday before the winter term at school started. They stayed at a delightful hotel in Rozel Bay and made good friends with the owners and members of their family, Arthur Sharpe, his wife and two small children, who were staying with them. The thing they enjoyed most was body surfing at St Ouen's Bay, which they did everyday, having a picnic lunch so they could spend the whole day there.

Val meanwhile, at home in England, was rushed into hospital to have her first child, two weeks early.

One morning, the sea was not good for surfing, so Moira said 'let's give up and try again this afternoon'. Tim aged eight, said 'just one more wave mummy' and they waited for the wave. It was the beginning of a freak sea. The wave was fifteen feet high and the force of it and the strength of the current was terrifying. It hit them and Tim disappeared in the water, arms and legs flailing. Moira managed to grab Nick, who put his arms round her neck and held on tight. When they surfaced, between waves, she told Nick to hold on to her swimsuit shoulder strap. He was instantly obedient, and there is no doubt that it helped save their lives. A woman standing up to her knees, at the edge of the sea, could not get out on to the shore and was screaming panic stricken. This set up the alarm. The four South African life guards were racing across the sand, pulled her out and then plunged into the huge waves to rescue Nick and Moira. Tim meanwhile had miraculously been swept on to the beach and safety. The life guards swam to Nick and Moira, two above water, two under alternately, and got to Nick. Moira knew that they would not be able to get them both to safety and gasped 'take the boy'. She then was virtually drowning. She was crying, because she thought Tim was dead and she said her prayers for Ted and her darling Val, and the new baby 'Tracey'. Then decided she would struggle for two more waves, and then just let go. Drowning is quite a gentle death and not fearful. The next thing she knew was strong hands grabbing her legs and body and then knew no more until she came round on the beach. Tim was crying and running round and round saying 'It's my mummy' Nick white faced and numb with cold, was told to run to the car to fetch towels and rugs, and the life guards worked on her to get the water out of her lungs.

Arthur Sharpe was wonderful. He took the boys under his wing and arranged for Moira to be taken to the hotel. She did not want to go to hospital, because she did not want Ted to know how near to disaster the whole episode was. It didn't stop Ted, from rushing to see Val in hospital on his way to Heathrow Airport and telling her inconsolably the terrible news. Val thought her mother was dead – a life for a life. Ted then flew to Jersey to be with his wife and children.

Moira was very strong and resilient and said she didn't want to spoil the holiday. She knew her friends, the Sharpe's would look after her, so Ted agreed to return to London.

When Moira was fit enough to go to St Ouen's again, she wanted to thank the brave young men from South Africa, who had saved their lives. She gave them some money, but how do you ever really repay the enormous debt you owe for your life. They shuffled their feet and one said, to cheer her up, 'We pulled another one out that afternoon!'

The freak sea had claimed several other victims round the coast of Britain, that day, and the Heath's were so lucky to have survived. Val had a rough time having her baby daughter, but all was well later on. Her second baby Kim, was born at Oakfield in 1963, in much happier circumstances.

Chapter 51

For the next few years, the band continued to enjoy great success. They were winning all the votes for the best band, the best male singer, the best female singer and the best individual instrumentalists, in the musical papers, The Melody Maker, The New Musical Express and the tabloid press, the Daily Sketch and the Daily Mirror. The trophies that Ted collected were considerable, and still adorn Moira's home to this day. A special and beautiful bronze is the Ivor Novello Award.

Incidentally, they were voted the most popular big band in 1997, by Big Band International. A wonderful tribute to these great musicians who carry on the Ted Heath Legend up to the present day.

Travelling a lot, working hard and enjoying their music, and building up an army of wonderful fans. They did three more tours of the States, but during the last of them, Ted was not at all well. In Chicago, he was very sick, and his loyal and caring band manager, Wally Palmer stood by at the side of the stage with a bowl, and Ted was continually having to go off stage to be sick. When he telephoned Moira that night after the show and told her how ill he was feeling, she immediately said she would fly out to look after him. He was adamant that she should not go. The weather was appalling with snow storms, and he said it would make him worse if he was worried about her safety. Sadly, they did not realise that this was a warning that Ted's health was failing. The years of hard physical work and late nights and travel, snatched meals, and the even harder stress on his mental well being were taking their toll. On top of that, business was becoming harder to get.

First there was 'skiffle' which Ted called Mickey Mouse music. It was played on washboards, and home made bass's and was the complete opposite to Ted's ideals of perfection and skilled musicianship.

Then the Roll 'n' Roll bands were becoming very popular, and taking a lot of Ted's audiences away. One concert the band was booked for was the out of doors Beaulieu Festival at Lord Montague's home, Beaulieu Abbey, after which Ted renamed a tune from the Australian Suite written by Kenny Graham, previously called 'Lovers on Bondi Beach'. It was one of Ted's favourite pieces. The audience was principally young, enthusiastic followers of the rock bands and especially of Acker Bilk, who was to finish the concert. During the Ted Heath Band performance, some of them started to chant "We want Acker, we want Acker" over and over again. Ted was pretty upset and back in the dressing room, during the interval, he felt unhappy and downcast. Acker Bilk came into his dressing room and told Ted he was just as upset about it as Ted was. He said he had always had enormous respect for Ted and all he had achieved with his music and he only wished he had been good enough to play in the Heath Band. A truly generous and kind gesture from one brilliant musician to another. Ted never forgot it.

Ted at Beaulieu in one of Lord Montague's vintage cars

Chapter 52

It was Easter time 1964 and Ted had been to see Fulham Football Club play. He sat in the director's box with Tommy Trinder, Chappie D'Amato, Lord Harewood and Charles Forte (later Lord Forte) and his young son Rocco. Nick, Tim and Moira were with him, and he enjoyed it all.

The next day was his birthday, 30th of March and he had to go down to Cardiff where the band were booked. For once, he was reluctant to go, and left home a little late. During his car ride to Paddington Station, he accidentally had a small bump with another car. He became very agitated about missing his train and told the other driver "You know who I am - send me the bill - I have a train to catch" and rushed off. He caught the train but was feeling ill and very tired. He dropped off to sleep, a deep sleep, and did not wake up until the station past Cardiff. In utter panic, he grabbed his case, dashed over the bridge to catch a train back. He was never late for a show - to him it was one of the cardinal sins. At Cardiff, he got in a taxi but collapsed on arrival at the dance hall. He was rushed into Cardiff Royal Infirmary in a coma.

Moira, at home, had an awful premonition that something was wrong. She had been wearing the pearl ring that Ted had given her for their thirtieth wedding anniversary. She took it off and put her beautiful engagement ring on, which she had worn all through the years. Superstitiously, she felt that pearls were for tears. Minutes later, the telephone rang to tell her of Ted's collapse. Val, Nick and Tim were with her and were towers of strength. Val telephoned British Rail and booked a sleeper for Moira to travel to Cardiff. She refused to let Moira drive down - packed her things and she, Nick and Tim took her to Euston Station. They told the night steward on the train that their mother was very distressed and asked him particularly to look after her. That night, Nick grew up. She arrived at Cardiff and went straight to the hospital. There, the news was not good. Ted was still in a coma, and the doctors were doing all they could. He had a massive blood clot in the main artery to the brain.

The nurses suggested she should check into a hotel, freshen up and return in the morning. She, however, wanted to be near Ted and after going to the hotel and booking a room, returned to the hospital and spent a night's vigil beside Ted's bed. After three days in a coma, Ted regained consciousness - Moira had been putting all her strength into willing him back to her, holding his hands close to her heart He was in a very agitated state, and wanted to go home immediately. The doctors persuaded him that he must rest a few more days, if he wished to recover. They were incredibly kind and understanding. Ted had always had a great fear of hospitals and death. In fact, he never went to funerals except his mother's. He used to send Moira in his place.

The hospital, a very old building, did not have any private rooms, and people visiting other patients, were naturally interested in looking into the ward to see Ted.

A gentleman, in the true sense of the word, Mr. Whitehead, leader of the Miners Union, was in the bed at the far end of the ward and had some privacy. Ted's bed was nearest the door. This very kind man suggested that Ted should be moved to his cubicle so the curtains could be drawn. He did not think people would be so interested in him. He was very seriously ill himself with a bad heart, but his caring and sympathy meant a great deal to Moira and they formed a friendship and talked long into the nights. He wrote a very sweet letter to Moira later sending her a silver miniature miner's lamp for luck.

Apart from returning to the hotel to change her clothes and bath, Moira was spending day and night at the hospital with Ted. The sister had arranged after a couple of days that she should eat at the hospital whenever possible. She held Ted's hand and willed with all her heart and soul that he would come back to her. With great thankfulness, at last he came out of his coma.

Arthur Askey, the famous comedian, was staying in the same hotel that Moira had checked into. On hearing of Ted's illness, he approached Moira, who was having a hurried snack, ordered a bottle of champagne and sat with her, doing everything he could to raise her spirits and make her smile. What a very kind and loving man, remembered with great affection.

Ted, however, became more and more irritable, and it was decided that it would be better for him to be moved to the Atkinson Morley Hospital in Wimbledon, which was adjacent to 'Oakfield'. A private compartment on the train to Paddington was reserved and an ambulance picked Ted and Moira up secretly from a back entrance of the hospital to take them to Cardiff station.

It must be said that the Press were never intrusive and treated Moira with the utmost courtesy and kindness. But Ted's illness was a news item of interest to their readers and they had their jobs to do. On the fifth day, they asked Moira to give them an interview. She asked them if they would mind meeting her in her bedroom at the hotel, so that she could put her feet up and rest, having had no sleep since Ted's collapse. They agreed and were kindness itself. One of them, from the Daily Mail, said to Moira "You are taking him home, aren't you". She felt guilty at not telling him that they were leaving the next morning but he wrote to her later and told her he fully understood. The press had always been kind to Ted and considerate and were never, ever unpleasant. The answer being, that if one treated them well, they reciprocated.

On the train to Paddington, Ted became more and more upset and vented his anger on Moira. The nurse, who was travelling with them, explained to Moira that the nature of Ted's illness made him very difficult and bad tempered and that it was going to be a very unhappy time for Moira. Ted, at that point, became quite violent, and went for the nurse. She suggested that Moira, who was by then in tears, should go to the buffet bar, while she coped with Ted.

When they arrived at Paddington, an ambulance with another nurse was waiting for them. Ted had been given a huge dose of sedatives to send him to sleep, but his strong will and determination beat them.

On arrival at Wimbledon, he became so upset at the thought of going into the Atkinson Morley hospital where a room was reserved for him, that the nurse and ambulance men decided not to risk him having a further stroke, and played for safety, and took him home. On arrival there, he immediately pushed them aside, rushed upstairs to the bathroom and locked himself in. There was only one thing to do. Val telephoned the hospital and asked them to send a nurse round, to look after Ted at home. They managed to calm him down, and get him into his own bed. From then on, three nurses were engaged to care for Ted. A morning nurse, an afternoon nurse and a night nurse. They were all marvellous and gentle, especially the night nurse, who had a gift of soothing him, and reassuring him. She read him poetry from Moira's collection of books and told Moira she could safely go to sleep with Val, in Val's bedroom and that she would call her if needed.

The next few weeks were very worrying and unhappy. Ted tried everything he could to escape the nurse's attention and was so dreadfully unhappy that he could not go to work. He took it all out on Moira and she was despairing.

Although the specialist, Jason Bryce, a good friend told her that Ted did not realise what he was doing, his personality had completely changed. Black was white, love was hate and the old saying 'You always hurt the one you love' was unhappily too true. He threw his food across the room, called Moira unspeakable names and life was unbearable. Tim, so young and gentle, said to Moira "You go and have a cup of tea mummy. I'll look after daddy. He isn't nasty to me". It broke Moira's heart.

Chapter 53

The musicians meanwhile had a meeting and decided that they would carry on with the engagements already booked, without a leader, until Ted could return to work. Kenny Baker took over some leading of the band, and Johnny Hawksworth too - in fact, they all pulled together not to let the 'old man' down. Jack Payne had offered to lead the band, but the musicians were sure the right thing to do was to carry on their own. Their loyalty and love for Ted and the band was out of this world.

Ted did finally recover enough to go to some of the radio sessions and later to lead the band again, but he was a very sick man. One of the early dates was the Red Feather's Ball at Cirencester. A smart charity affair. Ted was really not well, but delighted to be amongst his beloved musicians again. He had been told by the doctors, only to conduct the band for the first half of the evening, but like a naughty boy, he took his place on the stand, right in the middle of the brass players, grinning his head off and refusing to give up. It cheered him up no end, but gave Moira a worrying evening.

On the Decca recording session, which Decca and the B.B.C had arranged to celebrate the 21st Anniversary of the band, Ted, although very frail, stood in front of the band, but not realising that Ralph Dollimore, pianist and arranger to the band, was standing behind him conducting. It broke Moira's heart but the main thing was that he was so happy to be there.

It became very obvious that Ted was no longer able to honour his contract with Decca. But the arrangement over the years had been so good and strong (in the early years there was no contract, just a gentleman's agreement) that Decca and its American counterpart London Records , with Tony D'Amato did not want to be the ones to break it. Moira asked to see Hugh Mendle and Dick Rowe of Decca, to tell them that Ted was too ill to carry on. They were well aware of the situation but had wanted the break to come from Ted, and were so very sorry to cancel the contract as it stood. They did, however, continue to make records with the band.

From then on, Ted became progressively more and more ill. Thankfully, he was unaware of the serious nature of his illness, and was delighted when some of the musicians visited him at 'Moonridge' the house on the Wentworth Golf course, that they had moved to from Oakfield. The big house at Wimbledon, although the family home for so long, had become a heavy burden. Moira was afraid that she would not be able to manage a seventeen room house with a sick husband

and two young sons, without the domestic help they had previously been able to afford, and wanted a smaller house with less overheads. The only snag was that Ted wanted to live on a golf course, with a lot of land, and no close neighbours and fell in love with 'Moonridge'. It was a beautiful house but built for entertaining with three reception rooms, a huge kitchen, five bedrooms, two bathrooms, a swimming pool and six acres. Hardly the small house Moira had envisaged! A mini Hollywood.

Among their visitors were Harry Roche, who played golf there, and walked across their garden from the 18th hole, to see Ted, Jack Bentley and his lovely wife Wendy Craig, and most of all Dickie Valentine. Dickie. the dearest of friends who, when Ted finally went into hospital again , would ring up Moira, ask her what time she would be visiting Ted and offering to take her. He would sit beside Ted, holding his hand for a long time (although Ted no longer knew him) with tears in his eyes. A dear, dear friend

Moira had wanted to keep Ted at home as long as it was possible and for a time, after Ted had to go into hospital, had him home for tea and a light supper each day. He was happy then, and loved seeing Nick and Tim and Val and her two little daughters, Tracey and Kim, who treated him, like a beloved pet.

Sadly, one evening, he fell over and Moira could not get him up into a chair. It was a wet and windy day and nobody was on the golf course, which bordered the garden. Previously, if she had needed help, someone was always willing to come off the golf course and give her a hand, including the gardener from next door, George, a lovely man who was like a second father to Tim.

Moira put a cushion under Ted's head, covered him with a blanket and telephoned the hospital. They sent two nurses who took over, got him into the car, and she took him back to hospital. From then on, Ted could no longer go home. His condition deteriorated and he became more confused and bed-ridden. The nursing staff were kindness itself, and had grown very fond of him.

Moira visited him four times a day, the nurses said she was part of the furniture, and although he eventually appeared not to recognise her when she approached him, his eyes would flicker, and there was a slight pressure of his hand. She would dress up and put perfume on for each visit and she was sure he remembered the scent. She would also talk to him, and tell him all the news of home, the family and the music business. The nurses said he could not hear her or understand, but she was convinced it was important for her to treat him naturally, just in case, in that remarkable brain of his, was the need to be kept informed of everything and everybody he had lived his life for and loved.

After one serious bout of pneumonia from which he pulled through, he lived for another year, but in a vegetable state. To see and watch a man in such a pitiable state, whom she loved, was a tragedy for Moira, and she felt that the dreadful indignity of preserving life under these circumstances in a man who was a perfectionist in everything he did was a sin against humanity.

Moonridge, Wentworth – Ted's last home

Chapter 54

After several false alarms, the day came when the hospital called her urgently. She was alone - of all days, Val had gone to London, Tim to work in London, and Nick was at work in Kingston and Martin was abroad. So Moira was alone. The end was very near and for the first time for weeks, Ted's face was peaceful and calm. She told him that she loved him, and kissed him, and with a small sigh he was gone.

After five years of illness, the great Ted Heath was at peace.

The funeral was held at Slough Crematorium. It was a large chapel and Slough was accessible to the many people coming from London. The choice of music was very important. The lady organist was most helpful and wanted to know the family's choice well in advance so that she would have time to practice. With careful thought, they chose 'Panis Angelicas' for the beginning of the service. Don Lusher and the brass players of the band asked Moira if they could play during the service. They were in the musician's gallery and played at Moira's request 'Abide with me' very softly. The hymn Ted had played as a boy on Fulham Football ground.

Tears were pouring down many of the congregation's cheeks, it was so beautifully played, and very moving. The hospital chaplain, who knew Moira and Ted, gave the address and the service finished with the stirring and exciting Toccata by Widor. Moira and the family chose this particular piece of organ music, because they wanted everybody to go out with their heads high. Not one person walked out of the chapel until the music was finished. The lady organist played it brilliantly, a difficult task. The flowers were magnificent too, and the family took them to place in the hospital chapel, for the hospital staff and patients to enjoy their beauty.

Dickie Valentine spoke to Moira after the service, and said what a beautiful funeral it had been. He would like his funeral to be the same. Little did he know that it was not to be far off. His tragic death in a car accident came only fifteen months after Ted's. The musicians at Moira's request, played for Dickie too. Harry Roche, with typical musician's macabre humour, said, "We have given two auditions. Do we get the Job?"

It must also be mentioned that the undertaker for Ted's funeral was a great fan of the band. Without telling Moira, he had embalmed Ted and made his face up to look exactly as if he was going on stage. A kind tribute to a great musician from one of his many loving fans.

Chapter 55

There was a very dark chapter in Ted and Moira's lives. The memory of it has long been put away into the realms of forgetfulness, but it does not go away completely and was a deeply unhappy time.

Ted's intentions, all his married life, had been to protect, provide and give his wife and family security, if anything happened to him. Without realising it, due to his increasingly confused mind, all his plans for the future well being of the family, and most of his assets were disappearing and he and they needed help. Arthur Sharpe, their old family friend, who was a lawyer, said it really was necessary to apply to the Royal Court of Protection, as Ted was no longer able to manage to look after his affairs. This was done and the Court of Protection duly took over, albeit in a kindly way, but grievously sad. Ted's office in Hay Hill had to be closed and it devastated him to be told that he could not carry on his business and from then on his health rapidly deteriorated. The sad thing was that he was no longer well enough to work anyway. He was a lost soul.

In the recent years, since the band has been re-formed, under the direction of Don Lusher and with the original musicians, Moira feels sure that she has been guided by Ted, who appeared to her one night, some months after his passing, to prove his love. She knows that he is still there, watching, helping and being very proud of the legacy he left behind, the love for her, his family and his musicians has never died.

Foreseeing the future? Don Lusher behind Ted.

The Present Day

Chapter 56

After Ted's death, Moira had to move from 'Moonridge' and was fortunate to find a delightful little bungalow on the edge of the Wentworth Estate, which she named Christmas Cottage, a happy name. She found peace and happiness there, and only after ten years decided to move to be nearer Val, her daughter in Surrey.

There were some attempts to re-start up the band, but how could a Ted Heath be replaced? There were none that were right until Don Lusher, the great trombone player, who had worked with Ted, and had also formed his own band, who was willing and happy to revive the Ted Heath Band. The only stipulation by Moira, being that it was to be formed with Ted's original musicians.

There was no question that it should be a 'ghost' band with players who had not known or worked with Ted. This wonderful idea was a miracle in itself. The musicians were all keen and enthusiastic and, of course, being top class brilliant musicians, some of them band leaders in their own right, were playing as well as they ever did.

Don Lusher was the ideal choice as leader, dedicated with a heartfelt feeling of responsibility for taking on this wonderful band. His lovely wife Diana who was really too young to have known Ted, took on the huge task of sharing with Don, the behind the scenes work, that goes to making a band a success. Her help was invaluable. The library of Ted's music was packed in Moira's loft, but several scores and parts were missing, due to the previous attempts to revive the band, by Ralph Dollimore and Stan Reynolds, and the initial removal of the library from Ted's office to Ralph's flat, where it was found to be lying all over the floor, with some of the scores and parts missing.

Don would go over to Christmas Cottage, climb up into the attic and sort through the music. A mammoth and dirty task but he managed to find enough complete scores to play some concerts. Since then, of course, he has the music in his own safekeeping, and has had many missing parts copied from old recordings.

The reforming of the band came to the attention of Geoff Burdett of the National Westminster Bank, who is a big band buff. Nat West were prepared to sponsor the band at the Barbican, London and gave it the spur to do other concerts, especially at the Fairfield Hall Croydon, who were most supportive. The bank sponsored three highly successful concerts, three years running and for a time Geoff Burdett continued to promote concerts at various venues.

The main promotion of the band however was due to Derek Boulton, who not only promotes the concerts, but also puts up the money and produces the CDs and cassettes of the band's releases. There is much to be said about Derek. He was Ted's first ever band boy, playing hookie from school to work for Ted, fifty years ago, and he has been a loyal and loving friend ever since. Looking after Moira in every possible way, making her life easy and following Ted's dream of booking the band into first class hotels and first class travel and venues. He managed, amongst other great names, Tony Bennett for a long time, but his great love is the Ted Heath Band and the Heath family, for which they are forever grateful. Thanks are due too, to Siv, Derek's lovely wife, who does so much towards the organisation, publicity and booking of the band, and lets Derek spend so much time away from home, to attend concerts. She also supports not only him, but Arsenal Football Club, his obsession. Talking about 'spending' also reveals that Derek's hand is always in his pocket to see things run smoothly. To put it in a nutshell, he is the one who 'puts his money where his mouth is'

Don Lusher

Chapter 57

The following of the faithful fans have made it possible to do up to twelve concerts a year. The house full signs often go up and everybody is happy.

The line-up is a revelation. Jack Parnell drums, Kenny Baker trumpet, Tommy Whittle saxophone, clarinet and flute. Ronnie Hughes trumpet, all founder members of the band, Henry Mackenzie saxophone and clarinet, nineteen years in total until he retired, Ronnie Chamberlain soprano sax and alto, Roy Willox, later to be replaced by Ray Swinfield who had played in the latter years of Ted's band, a brilliant clarinet player, Eddie Mordue bass saxophone, Duncan Campbell trumpet and joyous laughter-maker, Derek Healey trumpet and second lead, Bill Geldard bass trombone and great arranger, Jackie Armstrong trombone and one of the early members of the band, Maurice Pratt trombone, later replaced on retirement by Ted Barker, Rick Kennedy, another early member, Norman Stenfalt pianist par excellence. Difficult to replace, but on his death Brian Dee stepped in, most effectively. With the band the whole time since it was reformed, Lennie Bush bass, who has become an intrinsic part of the rhythm section. These musicians are so special. There is no other band in the world like it, nor ever will be again. They are playing with their hearts, loving to get together for the concerts. It is like an old boy's club and any musicians who occasionally sit in with them, say it is an experience that they have never known with any other band. They bring out a special magic that leaves the many loyal fans and newcomers to the concerts with a feeling of exhilaration and total satisfaction.

Moira attends all the concerts. She has only missed two, for unavoidable reasons, and it is her great joy and pride to be associated with such wonderful musicians. The band plays exciting music from the Ted Heath library and adding to the nostalgic enjoyment, Dennis Lotis sings at every show. He and Jack Parnell travel huge distances to be with the band. Dennis lives with his lovely wife *Rena in Norfolk and Jack with Veronica in Suffolk. A long way to go to most of the concerts. In fact, the entire band travels long distances to be there.

These 'get togethers' are a source of happiness and affection. It proves how right Ted was, that it is important to have a band of musicians who like and support each other. Moira travels with Derek Boulton, or with Don and Diana. At the concerts, she is thrilled to be introduced by Don, as 'the lady who makes it all possible' and has the opportunity to meet the ever faithful fans.

There is also an extremely well run fan club, the Ted Heath Appreciation Society run by Pete Jones. They have regular meetings in London and there are several other societies formed around the country. People from South Africa, Australia, USA and Sweden attend some of the meetings when they are in England.

Pete does sterling work for the fan club, and produces an excellent magazine for the members. The other fan clubs around the country too, are very supportive. Especially Kyle Ferrier, the Kent branch, John Charman, West Surrey Big Band Society, Trevor Sadler and John Reason, West London and Peter Mouncey, York, the Windsor Big Bands and the Bournemouth Connection.

*Since writing this, Rena, Dennis' wife died – a great loss to him and all their friends. Rena was a gorgeous lady with a delightful sense of humour. A loving wife, a sweet and gentle mother of three sons, and a fascinating personality.

Dennis Lotis

Kenny Baker

Jack Parnell

Chapter 58

Nineteen Ninety Four was the 25th Anniversary of Ted's death. Moira thought it was time to consider having the finale. She met the band on stage at Portsmouth at the first concert of the year and told them of her decision. To a man they said a very firm "no". Jack Parnell said they were professional and would know when the time was right and the others all agreed. Tommy Whittle wrote a very charming letter to Moira saying he had been proud to be in the original band and enjoyed it, but if anything he was even prouder now, and enjoying it more. Moira was very touched at the reactions of them all, and has decided to leave all decisions to them. The band is still enjoying great success four years later. She would be very lost without her much loved musicians to whom she owes so much joy, and loves so much, and now says "Thank you".

So the Ted Heath story is not ended. Ted's music is still listened to by the ever-faithful fans and aficionados and in the concerts. Don Lusher and the musicians are delighted to see several young people in the audiences, who are thrilled and impressed to hear these great musicians playing their instruments with consummate artistry and without the aid of electronics instruments and computer conceived arrangements. Ted's signature tune 'Listen to my Music' says it all.

Tommy Whittle

Chapter 59

Moira now lives in a delightful terraced cottage, in Surrey, three doors from her beloved Val and gains great happiness and contentment from her full life. Attending all the concerts and giving an occasional record recital at the Ted Heath Appreciation Society meetings, the West Surrey Big Band Society, the Windsor Big Band Society, The Ted Heath Appreciation Society in Orpington, Kent and the Bournemouth Connection. All of which give her enormous pleasure and are well received by the fans.

She was very proud to be made a Freeman of the City of London in 1993 which she accepted as an honour for Ted - whose name was conspicuously absent from honours given to music makers by the then Government. In 1995 she was awarded the BASCA Gold Award at the Savoy for her part in keeping the wonderful Ted Heath Band going, an honour thanks to Don Lusher, the musicians and Derek Boulton who do all the hard work and are really the ones who make it all possible.

There is so much more to say, so many little anecdotes, so many occasions, so many laughs, so many tears, and more than anything else so many people, the friends and associates who played an important part in the lives of Ted and Moira. They are however not forgotten, and there follows a brief resume of these memories. If any have been left out, please forgive the omissions. Details and remembrances, as one gets older, fade and this book must be finished. But the enormous respect and love Ted and Moira received in their lives, is more than the heart can hold.

Nick, Val, Moira, Martin, Tim

Tim

Nick

Val and "Daisy Wilmot"

Ted

Recollections

LES BROWN

In 1951 Les Brown came over to England to play for the American Forces. He was with Bob Hope who did so much to entertain the American soldiers all over the world.

Les and Ted were keen to meet up again, but to no avail. They were both working every night. But Ted and Moira were due for a holiday. Moira was pregnant with Tim, their youngest and last child, and they had decided they would like to go to Venice again. Les Brown, quite determined that they should meet up said to Ted on the phone "why not catch up with us in Germany on your way to Venice". He obviously had not studied the map of Europe very thoroughly.

This was too much temptation for Ted to miss, so he hurriedly arranged passage and currency and off they set. They arrived in Wiesbaden just as the Bob Hope show was about to begin and sat down to enjoy the show. It was brilliant and for them to see Bob Hope working was an added bonus. From then on, Ted and Moira toured the first five days of their holiday with Les Brown and his Band of Renown and Bob Hope. They went on to Heidelberg, Nuremberg and Munich, and then decided they must sadly say goodbye. Moira was getting very tired.

They went on to Venice and enjoyed a peaceful time. Ted particularly was enchanted and intrigued by the huge orchestra playing in San Marco Square and some of their ancient instruments. They then visited Rome, and finished up in Cannes for a few days.

Years later, Les Brown and Claire, his charming wife came to London and stayed in the penthouse suite at the Dorchester Hotel. Les telephoned Moira and asked her to join them for afternoon tea, and spoke lovingly of Ted. A delightful man.

WOODY HERMAN

Whenever Woody came over to England, he always made sure that he and Ted got together. After Ted died, the friendship, if anything, became closer with Moira and he and Charlotte his lovely wife, always arranged to meet Moira. Charlotte would sometimes stay with Moira, while Woody continued on tour.

The first time they were over here, Ted and Moira invited Woody and Char for lunch on Good Friday at their Wimbledon house 'Oakfield'. Moira wanted it to be just right, so she chose the menu very carefully. It was cold Scottish salmon with cucumber sauce for a starter, roast lamb, new potatoes, peas and runner beans for the main course and summer pudding and ice cream for dessert. All was well for the first course, but when it came to the roast lamb, Woody delightfully and politely said to Moira "I guess you through I was Jewish" to which Moira blushingly agreed. Woody explained that they were Catholics, and the one, very special day in the year when they did not eat meat was Good Friday. Fortunately, the salmon was large and there was plenty left over, so they tucked into second helpings of it. Woody often reminded Moira of this episode with a twinkle in his eye.

When he and his band played at the Fairfield Hall, Croydon, Moira and Val were invited to the concert. Woody suggested that they joined him and Char at the Dorchester afterwards for supper.

They had gone in Moira's Triumph Herald convertible, her much loved little car, but rather old. It pelted with rain, and the soft hood leaked. Woody was highly amused at Moira's embarrassment and said he would not have missed the experience for the world. Of course, he was used to large luxurious American cars. He was a lovely man and a wonderful friend

MARLENE DIETRICH

When Marlene was to appear in Spain, she specifically asked for Ted's band to accompany her. Ted and Moira were walking from the hotel to the place where they were playing when there was a pitter patter of feet behind them, and a voice saying "Mr. Heath, Mr. Heath". It was Marlene. She put her arm through Ted's and said she was honoured to be working with him. Ted was knocked out.

When they got to the rehearsal, she found that the lights were not right, they had to be perfectly positioned, and the piano was in the wrong place too. This delightful lady, one of the greatest stars of our time, climbed a ladder to adjust the lights, speaking fluent Spanish, French and English to the electricians. Then when she was satisfied, she climbed down and proceeded to push the grand piano to exactly where she wanted it. She was fabulous and Ted and the musicians were entranced with this fascinating beautiful woman.

When she appeared in London doing her 'one man' show with Burt Bacharach, Ted and Moira went to see it. After the show, they went to the stage door, but there were so many people waiting to see her, Ted handed his visiting card to the stage door keeper, having written on it how much they had enjoyed the performance and sending her their love. They then walked off down the road, but the stage door man came running after them and said Miss Dietrich wanted to see them and would they return to the theatre. They were then shown to the stage, which had the curtains drawn back and the lights dimmed. They were asked to wait. After a short while she appeared, having changed into day clothes, taken her make-up off and looking exquisite. She went straight over to them, flinging her arms round them, and said "Darlings, how wonderful to see you". They talked for about ten minutes, then she said "goodbye" and moved on to other people waiting. Most stars let you visit them after a show in their dressing rooms, in their dressing gowns and with cold cream smothered over their faces to take off the make-up. Marlene was different. She added her own touch to the magic of a darkened theatre and stage, and gave a mystique to starry presence. A great star and a privilege to have known her.

LENA HORNE

Ted and Moira used to have a private joke, Ted saying, "If I were unfaithful to you, it would be with Lena Horne". Moira laughed and said "chance would be a fine thing! If I wcre unfaithful to you, it would be with Lord Louis Mountbatten". They were not to know that later on, not only did Ted work with Lena Horne at the London Casino but his and her dressing rooms were next door to each other. Moira swears she spent most nights at the Casino. Not really necessary, because they became good friends and Lena was a joy to know. Moira never did meet Lord Louis!

JOHNNY KEATING

One of the great names behind the Ted Heath Band was undoubtedly that of Johnny Keating. He was responsible for many of Ted's best numbers, his wonderful arrangements are never to be forgotten.

He would turn up at a session for a recording or broadcast, with the unfinished parts of a couple of numbers, requested by Ted. While the band ran through the early part of the arrangement, Johnny would frantically be finishing it off. Ted would sometimes be in despair, that he would never get the finished article, but lo and behold! Johnny achieved the miracle and a superb and beautiful arrangement was duly recorded and became a valuable addition to the band's repertoire.

Some of Johnny's work is close to genius – composer, musician, arranger and a delightful and loveable member of the Ted Heath Organisation. To him must go the recognition for a lot of the success of the band, and many thanks are due to this brilliant man.

Among the other arrangers that did sterling work for Ted, were Laurie Johnson, Alan Bristow, Reg Owen, Frank Horrox, Bill Geldard and of course Kenny Baker, Jack Parnell and Don Lusher, and many, many more

Little Recollections

Sammy Davis

When Ted was walking down to his office in Hay Hill, he suddenly heard a shout "Ted" and the next thing he knew was Sammy Davis Junior rushing up to him and jumping up with his arms round Ted's neck and his legs round his waist. At least he managed to stay upright and they had a good laugh.

Johnny Mathis

Johnny worked with Ted many times and they mutually admired each other's skill and professionalism. His letter to Ted, reproduced here, says it all:

Dear Ted

We had so little time to speak together. I want to take this time to tell you that never! and I have met all the people whom I have admired in show business, never have I met such a sweet gentleman in any business.

I had to come back to America to reminisce about the band and you.

The boys were the nicest I have ever met, and more co-operative than any anywhere.

I am trying to find a gift for you that is worthy of your character and goodness. It was indeed a pleasure for all concerned to be in your company.

I only hope that God will be gracious enough to grant us another meeting and an opportunity to be together.

It seems one must be deprived of surroundings and nice people to appreciate them.

Please know that we (Allyn, Jerry John Noga and everyone concerned) appreciated your kindness.

My love to your family and that <u>swinging band. They are dolls</u>

Hoping to see you again soon, I remain,
Johnny Mathis

A delightful and charming man.

Al Hibbler

On one of the American tours, the star guest was Al Hibbler. A great singer, with a marvellous sense of humour. One of the guys in the bus stripped down and made ridiculous faces to people outside, not, it must be said with Ted's approval but Al got to the front of the bus saying "This I must see", causing the musicians great amusement. You see, he was blind

Len Camber, *Geraldo's Vocalist*

When the Geraldo band were in Paris during the war, some of the guys thought it would be interesting to go to a classy Parisian brothel. There, the girls were thrilled to meet them and persuaded Len Camber to sing for them, He sang "I'll be seeing you in all the old Familiar Places" without trying to be funny.

Johnny Dankworth

Ted gave Johnny his first big break at one of the Palladium Swing sessions with the Johnny Dankworth Seven.

Johnny remembered it many years later when he made a guest appearance at the Barbican with the present band under the direction of Don Lusher. He played 'African Waltz' and was a great success.

People

Denis Chaundy

One of Ted's most ardent fans was a gentleman called Denis Chaundy. He spent all his spare time following the band and Ted called him his 'Number One Fan'! As a treat, Ted suggested that he should share the driving with Moira when she took the car to Germany, to meet Ted there for a tour of the American Air Force bases, including many very badly bombed cities, like Ulm, where the big railway junctions were and Kaiserslautern. Denis was caused some embarrassment when they boarded the car ferry at Harwich, to find they had been booked into a double cabin as Mr & Mrs Heath, but that was soon sorted out.

He and his charming wife, Rita, who attends the concerts in Birmingham to this day, even spent their honeymoon in Torquay, so Dennis could listen to the band every evening. Rita must have loved him very much.

When he died, many years later, he had asked for Ted's music to be played at his funeral. A faithful fan to the end.

Frank Lee

Frank Lee was the A & R (Artists and Repertoire) man at Decca. He supported the band to the full and was responsible for the 'Phase 4' albums. He was also responsible for the 'Baa-baa black sheep' in 'Swinging Shepherd Blues' one of Ted's great hits. He became a good friend over many years. When Ted was ill, he took Moira to see the ballet, which she loves, and showed her many kindnesses

Alan Dell

Alan was a very special man, the dearest of friends. Apart from his fantastic knowledge and dedication to big band music, there was so much more.

His beautiful, loving and caring nature was known to everybody in the music business. He never took, he always gave, he was a 'music man', not a 'money man'.

He fought hard to get as much air time on broadcasts with the BBC for British bands and at one time, he was told not to play so much British music, by the British Broadcasting Corporation! – He was infuriated and determined to continue his very valuable support. He had a huge room built on to his house, with all the equipment he needed to tape the reels and cassettes. He had a huge collection of tapes and he knew how to get the scratches out of old worn-out records.

Not to be forgotten is Alan's devoted and ever-loving wife Annie. Remembered with love and affection, she and Alan were a remarkable family couple. They adored their children and grandchildren. Alan's generosity of time for his professional life, his tactile hugs and kisses, were such a part of his nature, that they have left a lasting impression and memory of not only a 'music man' but of a family man too.

A great friend of modern swing music, and very much loved.

Malcolm Laycock

Since Alan Dell's death, his place as guardian, protector, lover of big band music and broadcaster, has been filled by Malcolm Laycock. He has his own individual style and is proving to be a great friend of musicians and a wonderful champion of British bands, generous with his time, courtesy and enthusiasm.

Other much valued supporters of the Big Bands, keeping them alive on the BBC are David Jacobs and Desmond Carrington.

Ronnie Scott

A great saxophone player and years after joked that he wasn't good enough to play in the Heath band but he made a great success of his life and founded the world renowned Ronnie Scott's Jazz Club

Peter Mouncey & Roy Elsworth

These are two stalwart members of the organisation, who must be mentioned too.

Roy Elsworth was originally a fan, but when Don needed a strong arm to help with setting up the stands for concerts, and collecting the music. Being an invaluable 'band boy' in many ways, Roy stepped in and is a wonderfully loyal 'prop' as well as a fund of knowledge.

Peter Mouncey, travels to the concerts and sells the programmes, besides running the fan club in York and giving recitals. His presence is always a delight, elegant and smiling and part of the Ted Heath 'family

Grandma – Ted's Mother

In 1926 there was a terrible General Strike, all transport was stopped. Ted lived at home with his parents in Wandsworth and went to the West End to work. Ted was devoted to his mother and father, and a very loving son. His father died just before Ted's marriage to Moira.

His mother lived at Oak Cottage with Ted and Moira and afterwards at Oakfield, for eleven years. She was never happier than being in the kitchen cooking for them (bread pudding was a favourite) but as she was getting older, she found the big house and the stairs too much for her. It was decided that she should live with Mrs Cunningham, one of the Heath's daily help's who lived nearby in Raynes Park. This proved to be a very happy arrangement. Mrs Cunningham's father was an ex brass band trombone player, but he had been gassed in World War One. He consequently had lost both legs due to gangrene. He and Grandma got on very well and her natural instincts to look after people had a perfect outlet.

She loved going to the cinema, the Rialto in Raynes Park for the afternoon performances. They served tea and biscuits for threepence. She lived with the Cunningham's , until the time of her death at the age of eighty two.

During those years, Ted sent her a weekly allowance. She got quite worried if it was a day late. But after her death, they found all the envelopes with the money in, unopened, hidden under the carpet in her bedroom.

Band Personnel

Some of the personnel of the band over the years, were:

Jackie Armstrong	Alan Franks	Don Lusher
Martin Ashton	Freddy Gardner	Henry Mackenzie
Kenny Baker	George Garnet	Mo Miller
Ted Barker	Bill Geldard	Eddie Mordue
Jack Bentley	Leslie Gilbert	Danny Moss
Eddie Blair	Max Goldberg	Kenny Napper
Greg Bowen	Dave Goldberg	Bobby Orr
Norman Burns	Ken Goldie	Reg Owen
Bob Burns	Jimmy Goss	Jack Parnell
Lad Busby	Charles Granville	Woolf Phillips
Lennie Bush	Johnny Gray	Freddie Phillips
Duncan Campbell	Harry Hall	Maurice Pratt
Ronnie Chamberlain	Johnny Hawksworth	Bobby Pratt
Pete Chilvers	Derek Healey	Red Price
Keith Christie	Frank Horrox	Frank Reidy
Kenny Clare	Ronnie Hughes	Don Rendal
Jimmy Coombes	George Hunter	Stan Reynolds
Bert Courtley	Norman Impey	Harry Roche
Ralph Dollimore	Ike Isaacs	Stan Roderick
Johnnie Edwards	Ric Kennedy	Johnnie Scott
Bob Efford	Ken Kiddier	Ronnie Scott
Bert Ezzard	Basil Kirchin	Ronnie Selby
Jack Fallon	Duncan Lamont	Jack Seymour
Victor Feldman	Harry Letham	Dave Shand
Tony Fisher	Bill Lewington	Ralph Sharon
Aubrey Franks	Vic Lewis	George Shearing

Charlie Short

Ronnie Simmons

Dave Simpson

Harry Smith

Wally Smith

Norman Stenfalt

Sammy Stokes

Ray Swinfield

Nat Temple

Cliff Townsend

Stan Tracey

Ronnie Verrell

Dennis Walton

Derek Warne

Tommy Whittle

Dave Wilkins

Roy Willox

Jimmy Wilson

Vocalists

Bobby Britton

Toni Eden

Kathy Lloyd

Dennis Lotis

Peter Lowe

Lydia Macdonald

Lita Roza

Dickie Valentine

Please forgive any omissions the passing of many years, and old age creeping on treats the memory with little respect - sorry.

Ted's Cars

Ted loved his cars, but did not have much idea of mechanics and that a car needed a little more tender loving care than copious helpings of petrol when necessary, and car washing and polishing to keep it shiny.

One of his first cars was a Sunbeam Talbot, a super little car, which took Ted and Moira all over France and the mountains, and throughout their courting days.

His next car was the Buick, mentioned previously.

Then his war time car, a rather Heinz 57 variety but sturdy, reliable and economical to run. He was allowed petrol to run this car, because the job of being in Geraldo's was considered to be of national importance.

After the war he had a Wolseley which faithfully took him to football matches when Fulham were playing away, and of course to work

The next car was a fantastic Armstrong Siddeley built like a bus, pale green, with green leather upholstery and very smart but expensive to run. A classic car, but big.

He also bought a car in Scotland, had it sent down to London by train and the first time he drove it, the engine started making noises like hundreds of chickens clucking, which caused astonished looks from passers-by. He got his friend, George Ratcliffe, the saxophone player to take it off him and sell it. When Raddy was delivering it to a buyer, the gear broke off in his hand, in the middle of Tooting Broadway and so that car proved to be a total loss.

Moira, meanwhile had bought a new Hillman Minx convertible from her share of the royalties of 'I'm Gonna Love that Guy' - literally for a song. It was a super little car and Ted enjoyed driving it over the Alps, through the Susten Pass and over the St. Gothard Pass in Switzerland. In fact he enjoyed driving it more than the Armstrong Siddeley, and made Moira drive that while he drove the Hillman. Moira persuaded him to buy a brand new car instead of second-hand ones, so he bought a Humber Super Snipe, which was a wonderful car, and the joy of Ted's heart.

Finally, he decided to go up in the car world even more and bought a Jaguar Mark 8, which was beautiful. His last car was another Jaguar, a Mark 9. He had it sprayed a pale metallic green like a Bentley, and was very proud of it. His first Jaguar had a special number. The garage where he bought it had decided he should have a cherished number. At that time they could have got him TOP10, but he turned it down saying it would make him feel "a Charlie", so he had TH8 which was more to his taste. It was kept on for his second Jaguar and then Moira had it on her Triumph, and lastly on her little purple mini, only to let it go when she needed a new car and it virtually paid for a new Fiesta, which she kept for ten years.

Ted was heartbroken when he could no longer drive, due to his illness and really hated being driven by anyone else. Moira drove well, but Ted was not a happy man and it upset him greatly to feel helpless in his beautiful car. Moira used to drive him down to Millfield School in Somerset, where Nick was a pupil, and to her amusement, the boys would say 'Look here comes the driverless car' because she was rather small. One such visit, they were on their way home across Salisbury Plain, the weather was snowy and the ground icy. In the middle of Salisbury Plain, Moira stalled the engine. She and Ted got out of the car, to look at the engine, neither knowing anything about car engines, then Ted said 'You silly woman! I am going to drive'. Moira told Tim to sit in the back, and to her fear and trepidation, Ted drove triumphantly for two miles, until they reached civilisation

He would, too, have liked to have a Rolls Royce, but felt he never could afford it. Let it be remembered though, that he was a brilliant driver and drove many musicians home after a gig, and enjoyed the thousands of miles of driving. How he would have loved the motorways too, getting from A to B without stopping, not even for a 'wee wee'!!

Holidays

Ted never really wanted to take holidays, but Moira insisted that he must have a break from work. A futile wish really because he would spend hours in the hotel bedroom, studying the form book to pick out horses and then ringing up London over and over again.

They did visit some lovely places though.

In the early years of their marriage, they rented a bungalow in Bigbury, Devon and Ted did relax. They ate when they were hungry, slept when they were sleepy and played golf every day. They had a small dinghy, which proved great fun for Ray, Bobby, Martin and Val. When Ted decided he would show them how to manoeuvre it, he went round and round in circles, until he collapsed in the bottom of it, faced with hysterical laughter from his children.

After the war, he and Moira went to Switzerland, their first holiday for years. They stayed in Zurich at the Dolder Grand Hotel. While they were listening to Nat King Cole singing 'Nature Boy' on record. Nicholas was conceived. Ted was over the moon. Moira had wanted to work in the property market – She felt her brain was turning into cotton wool, but Ted did not want his wife to work so a new young family was a perfect way to keep her at home.

They spent one holiday in Fuengirola in Spain. Still, at that time, a very quiet unspoiled place. They stayed at a charming old hotel, overlooking the beach. It was furnished with antiques, including a large four poster bed and indeed was very antique altogether. The lights failed every night, candles had to be lit and Ted was bored out of his mind, no telephone, no car. He would stand at the gates, watching the cars go by, desperate to get back to civilisation. They went on to the Castellana Hilton in Madrid – civilisation at last.

The first night they were there, all the lights failed, just as Ted was shaving, before dinner. There was a candle, but as they were both non-smokers, they had no matches and were left in the dark – so much for civilisation!

Another holiday, was spent in Casteldafels, near Barcelona. They hired a car, which enabled Ted to drive to the airport everyday to collect the English newspapers, principally for the sports pages! This car had a manually operated gear change, something Ted was not used to, after the luxury of his Jaguar automatic. Driving through Barcelona city centre was horrendous. There were trams and mad continental drivers. On one occasion, he jammed the gears and stalled the engine in the middle of the worst of the traffic. His frustration knew no bounds, and he told his giggling family to 'Stop that cackling' which made them giggle all the more.

Ted and Moira spent a delightful holiday in Venice. The holiday had started, at the drop of a hat while touring in Germany with Les Brown and Bob Hope. The only way Ted and Les could meet as previously mentioned. They drove across France and into Germany, where Les and Bob were playing, in Weisbaden. They then toured on to Heidelberg, Neuremberg and Munich. Beautiful country and a wonderful experience seeing Les Brown and his band of Renown, and Bob Hope work. Bob's timing and sheer expertise was a revelation and of course Les Brown's band was terrific.

Moira was pregnant, and the busman's holiday was proving to be a little tiring. They left the road show reluctantly with fond farewells. Bob Hope calling Moira 'Little Mom', and having made a lasting friendship with Les. They then continued their previously planned holiday, Milan, Rome and then on to Venice.

Venice in May was delightful, except when St Mark's Square was flooded with the high tides. The famous smell was overwhelming, especially for a pregnant lady. They were fortunate enough to be staying in a hotel off the square, and had a penthouse apartment, which was high enough to be away from the stench. They were a little worried about the expense of their accommodation, so they would buy delicious fresh bread, beautiful cheeses and a bottle of wine. Take it secretly up to their luxurious suite and enjoy it rather guiltily, carefully brushing up any crumbs they had dropped. Ted was entranced by the huge orchestra that played in the square, and prowled among the musicians, intensely interested in their ancient instruments.

Years later, they returned to Venice, but this time stayed on the Lido at the Hotel des Bains. This hotel was the one where the Dirk Bogarde film 'Death in Venice' was filmed. An exquisite place, with a tunnel under the road to the beach. There they had a cabana, and Moira, Val, Nick and Tim spent the days on the beach and enjoyed the wild strawberries that were offered to them.

Ted, meanwhile, spent most of the time in the bedroom studying the form book and ringing London. His idea of a good holiday!

They did go, most evenings on a boat to Venice and the children had ice creams and fed the millions of pigeons. They also went sailing a few times.

They went to Cannes in the spring, when it was quiet and out of season. They stayed at a delightful hotel, a converted old mansion on the Croisette called the Hotel Grey d'Albion, with enormous rooms and bathroom, but no dining room, so they ate out at the many restaurants in the town.

When they were on the beach, the prostitutes from Paris would be perfecting their tans before their busy season. Ted would say to Moira, 'Do you mind if I watch them?' and he would lie on his stomach and feast his eyes on these beautiful creatures. One especially, who wore only small violets in strategic positions, he found particularly fascinating!

They returned several times to Cannes. Once on the drive to the South of France, they stayed in a little place called Eze for the night. During the night, a huge cicada (grasshopper) jumped through the window of their bedroom. Ted was terrified, and pulled the bedclothes over his head. Moira had to do something positive, otherwise there would be no sleep that night. She grabbed the chamber pot from under the bed, and put it over the cicada, which rattled for a while and then there was peace. The next morning, she removed the chamber and the large insect jumped out of the window unharmed.

They took the family to Cannes one year, and stayed at the same hotel as before. The maid loved Nick and Tim, little blonde blue eyed boys and every evening said 'Bonne nuit' to them. They thought it was her name and from then on she was called 'Bonne Nuit'.

The film 'To Catch a Thief' starring Cary Grant and Grace Kelly (late Princess Grace of Monaco) was being shot there at that time and Val was very thrilled to meet Cary Grant, the great film star

Tribute on Albums

Written by Moira.

Ted was essentially a quiet man – gentle, kind and in the beginning, very shy and retiring. The loud exciting, aggressive sounds of his music were his alter ego. The soft deep quality sounds would sometimes almost reduce him to tears.

He loved his work, beyond anything else in his life. What a wonderful joy for a man to have been able to work at what he loved best, with the people he knew and cared for, to achieve the heights of success in his profession and to be remembered with love and affection by so many.

He dreamed a dream, and the dream became reality.

The Ted Heath Band, directed by Don Lusher

Ted, Ric Kennedy, Wally Smith, Don Lusher, Jimmy Coombes

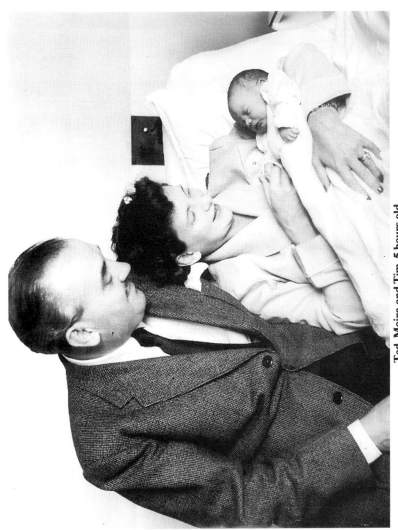

Ted, Moira and Tim, 5 hours old

Epilogue

Tears do not fulfil the need of love, physical or deep emotion

Tears are not the answer dear, dear one to the question of

devotion

But if my tears can join yours and through the long, long night

We Cry!

Before the light for one sweet moment

Perhaps we'll lie together –

I try not to think about you,

Put you out of my life forever,

Yet we shed our tears tonight,

My darling and we are together.

10 p.m. December 18th 1970

Found by Val amongst old papers of Moira's and forgotten all these years – It was written two days after Ted and Moira's 37th wedding anniversary, and 13 months after Ted's death.

The Band, present-day, at rehearsal

Index